The secrets of success in management

20 ways to survive and thrive

Andrew Leigh

PEARSON

Prentice Hall

BUSINESS

Harlow, England • London • New York • Boston • San Francisco • Toronto
Sydney • Tokyo • Singapore • Hong Kong • Seoul • Taipei • New Delhi
Cape Town • Madrid • Mexico City • Amsterdam • Munich • Paris • Milan

PEARSON EDUCATION LIMITED

Edinburgh Gate
Harlow CM20 2JE
Tel: +44 (0)1279 623623
Fax: +44 (0)1279 431059
Website: www.pearsoned.co.uk

First published in Great Britain in 2009

© Pearson Education Limited 2009

The right of Andrew Leigh to be identified as author of this work has been asserted by
him in accordance with the Copyright, Designs and Patents Act 1988.

ISBN: 978-0-273-72034-8

British Library Cataloguing-in-Publication Data
A catalogue record for this book is available from the British Library

Library of Congress Cataloging-in-Publication Data
Leigh, Andrew.
  The secrets of success in management : 20 ways to survive and thrive / Andrew Leigh.
    p. cm.
  ISBN 978-0-273-72034-8 (pbk.)
  1. Executive ability. 2. Management. 3. Success in business. I. Title.
  HD38.2.L445 2009
  658.4'09--dc22
                        2008036244

10 9 8 7 6 5 4 3 2 1
12 11 10 09 08

Text design by Sue Lamble
Typeset in 10 pt Iowan Old Style by 30
Printed and bound in Great Britain by Henry Ling Ltd, Dorchester, Dorset

The publisher's policy is to use paper manufactured from sustainable forests.

The secrets of success in management

Contents

About the author   vii
Acknowledgements   ix
Introduction   xi

PART 1 **Manage yourself**   1

   1 Cultivate emotional intelligence   3
   2 Listen actively   15
   3 Handle stress   31
   4 Give powerful presentations   43
   5 Network actively   57
   6 Write with impact   69

PART 2 **Manage others**   83

   7 Show leadership   87
   8 Manage your team   99
   9 Manage your boss   113
  10 Review performance   123
  11 Coach for results   135
  12 Negotiate successfully   149
  13 Manage problem people   161

PART 3   Manage the organisation   175

14   Manage time and goals   177
15   Manage change   191
16   Make decisions   205
17   Inspire meetings   219
18   Encourage creativity and innovation   231
19   Select and recruit   243
20   Persuade and influence   257

Last word   271
Sources   273

About the author

ANDREW LEIGH is author of over a dozen books on management, many translated around the world. They deal with teams, leadership, presenting, change, communication, decision making and, most recently, charisma (see **www.charisma-effect.com**).

Originally trained as an economist, he has an MA in the field of Human Resources, and is a Chartered Fellow of the Chartered Institute of Personnel and Development.

Andrew started his working career in marketing, later joining *The Observer* newspaper as a business feature writer. His regular newspaper column on Social Services led to a natural move into local government, where he established and managed a large research and development unit in a London local authority. On becoming Assistant Director of Social Work, he led a diverse range of teams, concluding his period in the public sector by setting up and managing a large Adult Service division with over 1000 staff and numerous residential homes and day centres.

With his fellow director Michael Maynard, Andrew founded Maynard Leigh Associates in 1989, now a leading UK development company specialising in helping clients achieve behavioural change at the individual, team and corporate levels. The company's clients include Aviva, Barclaycard, DHL, KPMG, Ernst & Young and Visa.

As a consultant, Andrew advises companies on creating effective people development programmes, particularly ones dealing with cultural change.

Contact him at **www.maynardleigh.co.uk**.

Acknowledgements

Special thanks to Aiden Leigh, Ainun Ayub, Michael Maynard and Gillian Leigh for their editorial contributions to this book.

Thanks also to Darion Leigh for assistance with graphics, Samantha Jackson from Pearson who steered the book through to publication and Nick Hine of Thomas Eggar for giving permission to use him as a networking case study.

The Secrets of Success in Management is dedicated to Amy-Jayne.

Publisher's acknowledgements

We are grateful to the following for permission to reproduce copyright material:

Table 1.1 from *Emotional Intelligence in Action*, Pfeiffer (Hughes, M., Bonita Patterson, L. and Bradford Terrel, J. 2005). Reprinted with permission of John Wiley & Sons, Inc.; Figure on page 17 from *Messages: Building Interpersonal Communication Skills*, Allyn & Bacon (De Vito, J.A. 2005); Figure on page 70 © White Smoke Software; Figures on pages 102, 111, 136, 139 and 140 © Maynard Leigh Associates; Figure on page 125 © Institute for Employment Studies.

In some instances, we have been unable to trace the owners of copyright material and we would appreciate any information that would enable us to do so.

Introduction

IN MY IMAGINATION, I HAVE a film running through my head. In it, a new or recently appointed manager picks up *The Secrets of Success in Management* and experiences a tingle of excitement on realising, 'Hey! This is really useful stuff!'

The film continues with this person handing on the book to a colleague, urging: 'You have to read this, it's gold dust!' Well, that is my dream anyway. This is certainly meant to be the sort of book I wish I had found when starting as a manager – stuff I could use, as I struggled to switch on other people to do their best, to do what I wanted them to do.

You are on an exciting, creative and rewarding journey, becoming a successful manager. Like anyone embarking on a lengthy trip, it is worth taking some essentials with you. While not exactly a manual of how to manage, consider this book as more like a compass, or a reassuring traveller's kit to support you along the way.

In my most recent incarnation as a manager, running my own company, it's as close as you can get to herding cats. All our consultants are strong-minded, insightful, self-reliant, audience-hungry, occasionally disorganised, successful actors. They use their special skills to assist tough-minded, sceptical business people to examine and alter their behaviour, affect corporate cultures, and rediscover their enthusiasm and ability to make a difference.

Attempting to steer this unique group of knowledge workers towards our own business goals seems at times doomed to failure. Directing them has proved every bit as challenging as managing social workers, staff in a dozen homes for the elderly, or steering a team of several hundred home helps.

The Secrets of Success in Management therefore contains tips, ideas and know-how that nobody usually bothers to share with you when you start out as a manager. Many are obvious, apparently common sense, yet so much of modern management seems devoid of this vital ingredient, swamped by jargon, unnecessary complexity or a straight understanding of the essentials.

One of the most satisfying aspects of being a manager is making a difference, realising that you can indeed make things happen. With experience, you will gradually master the role, uncovering ever more ways to get things done.

with experience, you will gradually master the role

Depending on your background, an early challenge may be making the switch from being a valued professional, where everything depends on personal output and performance, to managing others.

Understanding the differences between professional versus manager can affect how easily you adjust to the new role.

A professional...	A manager...
Keeps people informed	Positions self as a leader
Investigates	Does research
Tells people what to do and sets limits	Demands high performance
Communicates clearly	Acts to make things better
Understands the climate and culture	Understands the politics
Provides reasons	Provides feedback
Has a positive attitude towards the team	Solicits input
Improves performance	Sets challenging goals
Explains	Engages

This book aims to help make sense of your role, by focusing on the key essentials – the core of what being a manager is about.

The tools delusion

'Just give us the tools and we will finish the job,' Winston Churchill once famously demanded, and it is easy to imagine that managing effectively simply means having the right tools to hand. You will certainly never run short of potentially useful ones to help you manage. A detailed 2007 study by Bain & Company identified 100 tools that managers rated as high and used often, such as Client Relations Management, to those they rated as low and hardly used at all, such as Corporate Blogs. Yet it takes more than techniques to traverse the performance maze successfully and make your mark as a manager, which is what this book aims to help you do.

Becoming a manager for the first time will usually be a pivotal career experience and, in the right organisation, will stretch you to the limit. Just to put this in perspective, studies suggest that within the first 18 months of their new appointment, around 40 per cent of starter managers receive a bad review, voluntarily step down from their positions or lose their jobs. As the high turnover of CEOs shows, even the top slot seldom offers a safe haven.

Using this book should enable you to navigate your way through the minefields, quicksand and reefs that lie waiting for the unwary. It may also help if you can find a trustworthy mentor or a coach able to support you in your new challenge.

They need you to succeed

The good news is that you start with a built-in advantage! Most organisations desperately need their managers on the front line to succeed, relying on them to sustain quality, service and innovation.

Another advantage you possess is that outstanding managers – and you can certainly be one of them – produce disproportionately more value than the average, pedestrian manager. And anyone consistently adding value will soon prove suitable for further promotion.

But first, you must survive in this new role. In most busy managerial jobs, you could probably sit at your desk and do little, since soon the phone rings, an e-mail pops up, someone comes in wanting help or there are meetings to attend, lots of them. Quickly your day fills with activity you never initiated, giving the illusion you are doing something of value.

first, you must survive in this new role

What your organisation needs though is for you to be proactive, to rise above the maelstrom of busyness that engulfs people in most organisations and start to make a difference. If all you desire is a quiet life, this is probably not the best book to read right now!

Beginner traps

Trap 1 – the allure of power

'If only I could move to the next level I could do so much more,' is a siren sound you might hear in your head. Many who decide to try their hand at managing feel this allure of acquiring more authority and freedom. Yet experienced managers find that each promotion brings its own constraints, creating more, not less, dependency on others.

Trap 2 – 'me' not 'we'

Writing about a famously self-important Mayor of New York, a journalist summed him up in terms of 'Enough about me! Let's talk about you. What do you think of me?' Once you become a manager, it is time to stop using 'me' or 'I' and instead start using a 'we' mentality.

Trap 3 – the DIY temptation

Imagine you are one of those handy people able to fix anything – creaky doors, cracked light switches, worn tap washers. Naturally, the jobs keep coming and if you allow it, you could spend most of your time as a fixer. But sometimes it makes more sense to call in a plumber, or hire someone for a job you can personally do, but which frees you to do something more worthwhile.

Similarly at work, because you know the answers and can get results faster by going it alone, your natural response to meeting deadlines, solving problems, getting results and ensuring quality may be to do-it-yourself.

But this DIY temptation is a trap. Instead, your new role requires you to be willing to call in the equivalent of the plumber, since it will free you to do something more useful, such as thinking, networking or staying in touch with your boss.

Trap 4 – emotional reactions

doubts may start to surface

Think back to when you first learned of your new management job. How did you feel? Elated, daunted, excited, or worried? Most people initially experience some kind of positive emotional reaction at the prospect. But when the dust starts to settle, doubts may start to surface:

◆ **Am I good enough?** 'Can I really do this thing? Do I really have what it takes?' You are right to wonder about this. If you do not, then like an actor marching on stage without a shred of fear, you have probably not fully attuned to the forthcoming challenge. Be assured your boss feels the same way, and their boss too. Right to the top self-doubts remain, no matter how successful the person appears in public.

- **Loss of status:** 'Other people will now get the credit for achievements and build their profile, rather than mine.' Now you gain status or profile through the success of others working for you. Their successes become your successes.

- **Loss of control:** 'I know how this task or project needs to be done, so must supervise colleagues closely' or 'I need to read every e-mail that comes my way'. If you want your people to feel accountable, you need to get out of the way, rather than seek control. This does not mean abandoning your people to their own devices. Instead, show you are readily available for advice and support. Saying, 'My door is always open to you,' is not enough, and probably means the opposite. Instead, show your people you can be readily contacted, and remain highly visible.

- **Loss of friendships:** 'I don't want to lose my good relationships with former peers.' Anxiety about losing friendships with former peers, though understandable, can potentially undermine you. You may try too hard to keep them happy, encouraging them to believe they can have an easy ride. The solution is to do what is right, always being scrupulously fair. Also, let them realise you now act as their ambassador, making your people your priority.

Three priorities

In the early days of managing, much well-meaning advice may flood in, and it can be hard to define the priorities. Your job description may be full of tasks and responsibilities but, apart from the basics of getting to know your people and what makes them tick, where do you start?

Pursue performance issues

It seldom takes long. Often within weeks or days of becoming a manager, you will probably start to encounter performance issues. Non-delivery, late delivery, the wrong delivery, personality clashes affecting performance, poor work attendance, low motivation, may all rapidly surface as you get to grips with the new role.

What exactly do you do? The temptation can be to hope matters will magically improve. Rather than risk confrontation, unpleasantness or loss of friendship you stay frozen in inaction. Inaction, though, soon turns performance issues into a credibility problem. People start wondering about your own commitment to performance and to being action-minded.

Tackle performance issues when they arise. You may need to tread carefully, but at least start to tread, not stopping until you nudge performance back on track. Once people see you as decisive in this area, the word soon spreads and tackling the next occurrence will be easier.

In your keenness to tackle performance issues though, use the rule of thumb – 'seek first to understand' – before plunging in and assuming someone is falling down on the job. (See also Chapter 10.)

Treat your boss as a friend

So you think your boss is inept, arrogant or just plain lazy? You are not alone. A Gallup Poll in 2007 found that a bad relationship with the boss was the Number 1 reason people gave for leaving their jobs. But if you want to keep moving up the corporate rungs, never treat this person as an enemy. It seldom works as a survival tactic let alone as a route to success.

If you try to stay under the boss's radar, avoid drawing attention to yourself, or keep your head down you may merely create anxiety and that is no way to treat a friend. It is also a sign of strength, not weakness, to ask for advice, support and a clear statement of what the boss expects of you. Assume your boss is on your side and act accordingly. (See also Chapter 9.)

View from the top

Those at the top of their organisation usually develop their own list of what led to success. You will eventually arrive at your own, but here are some of the essentials.

Obtain the best information possible

Once you have this information then trust your instinct and make a decision. When joining the highly regarded US Nordstrom retail company, new recruits receive a book entitled *Rules of the Organisation*. Inside it is blank, except for this:

> **Rule #1: Use your good judgment in all situations.**
>
> **There will be no additional rules.**

The organisation pays you to use your judgement, which means taking decisions when you cannot be sure you are right. At Toyota, employees have the freedom to make judgement calls while adhering to a broad set of guidelines, rather than following a strict set of rules.

Inexperienced managers often suffer from the paralysis of analysis. This arises from the fruitless search for sufficient information to make judgements fireproof. You will always either have more information than you can handle, or never quite enough!

Really get to know your team

'Put more effort and time into this than you really want to. Talk to them and listen, even when you know what you are hearing is wrong,' argues Dennis Stevenson, the Chairman of Pearson. Alan Leighton, Royal Mail's Chairman puts it equally forcefully:

> *'The first 100 days are key: manage your team, listen to them and remember to get 70 per cent right you have to get 30 per cent wrong.'* (*On Leadership,* 2008)

(See also Chapters 2 and 8.)

Build relationships

Most successful managers will tell you how important it is to invest in relationships. As David Ogilvy, founder of Ogilvy & Mather put it: 'No matter how much time you spend thinking about, worrying about, evaluating people, it won't be enough.'

Building relations may hardly seem the essence of management science or a tangible 'how to' technique of management. Yet those at the top have usually spent countless hours on understanding, rewarding and relating closely to people.

Making sense of this book

The Secrets of Success in Management deals with the three basic areas of successful management: managing self, managing others and managing the organisation. Within these three groups are the 20 key management processes all successful managers need to master.

Manage self
◆ Cultivate emotional intelligence
◆ Listen actively
◆ Handle stress
◆ Give powerful presentations
◆ Network actively
◆ Write with impact

Manage others
◆ Show leadership
◆ Manage your team
◆ Manage your boss
◆ Review performance
◆ Coach for results
◆ Negotiate successfully
◆ Manage problem people

Manage the organisation
◆ Manage time and goals
◆ Manage change
◆ Make decisions
◆ Inspire meetings
◆ Encourage creativity and innovation
◆ Select and recruit
◆ Persuade and influence

This book focuses on people, because it is they who ultimately make organisations succeed, rather than say capital, technology, budgeting or building a business plan.

Unfortunately, no individual comes complete with a manual showing how you get the best from them. To manage all three groups – self, others and the organisation – you need to develop your natural insight.

Insight

insight can seem magical if you are on the outside

Can anyone become an insightful manager? Is it something you are born with or can you develop this ability? Insight can seem magical if you are on the outside looking in. But from the inside it is simply based on heightened awareness, which you can certainly systematically develop. Awareness stems from acquiring information, observing and becoming more conscious of self, others and the organisation.

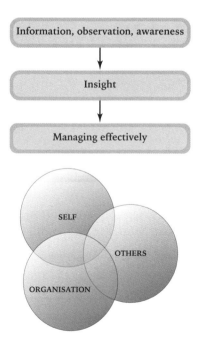

It is a real compliment when people regard you as insightful. They see you as someone with judgement, understanding and foresight.

◆ Managing self, or awareness of self, requires you to stay awake, and apply your insight to how you can grow and develop as a person.

◆ Managing others requires you to become aware of what others need to be effective and applying your insight to helping them perform at their best, unlocking their potential.

◆ Finally, managing the organisation requires you to become aware of the situation, and use your insight to make the impact you want.

Identifying your priorities

Since the purpose of this book is to trigger action, where do you start? You cannot immediately pursue everything set out here. Instead, you may find it more useful to keep returning to pick up new ideas over the coming months, as you encounter new situations. It is, therefore, unnecessary to read every chapter or go through the entire book in sequence. Instead, you can focus on those areas most relevant to your immediate development.

To help you decide on the priorities for your development there is a specially developed online questionnaire that you can use right now. It will analyse which chapters you should read first, and which you can probably leave until later. You will find the tool at: **www.20ways.dpgplpc.co.uk.** When you use this diagnostic tool, it will also suggest further reading associated with each of the recommended chapters.

On the website you can also access the entire further reading list for all 20 chapters. The list includes books and articles and the occasional website that you may find useful when following up your reading here. Based on your priority reading I am going to assume you will take some practical action. The choice of action naturally remains entirely up to you.

After using the online questionnaire you will automatically receive a three-month follow-up invitation to assess how you are doing in using the material from the priority chapters. Hopefully this will provide a further incentive to take action.

The best way

'Management is out of date,' complains Gary Hamel, writing about its future, 'Like the combustion engine it's a technology that has largely stopped evolving...'. Yet you have not stopped evolving, you need not be out of date nor ineffective.

No one best way to manage exists, nor would such a holy grail be credible. But there are certainly some basic principles for doing the job well and this book provides them for you to consider and explore. You do not need to feel burdened by hierarchies, overwhelmed by the bureaucracy or disempowered by work pressures.

there are certainly some basic principles for doing the job well

There is nobody insisting you read every e-mail or attend every useless meeting.

To manage well, first decide to manage yourself, taking the responsibility to be proactive. From there you can move on to managing others and then finally figure out how to affect the organisation.

I can't say that I have loved every minute of being a manager, and have experienced some hopeless bosses along the way. Yet, like others who have survived and thrived in this role, I have gained a great deal from it, met some terrific people and, above all, made things happen.

If you want more, it is there for the taking.

PART 1

Manage self

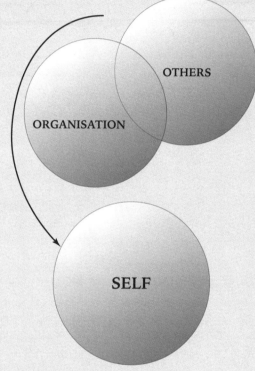

Self

- ◆ Cultivate emotional intelligence
- ◆ Listen actively
- ◆ Handle stress
- ◆ Give powerful presentations
- ◆ Network actively
- ◆ Write with impact

Peter Drucker, the doyen of management whose insightful observations about the subject still resonate around the world, once argued that executives ought to apply their managerial skills to their own lives not just their jobs and careers.

Managing self, or awareness of self, requires you to stay awake and apply your insight to growing and developing as a person. Naturally this covers all aspects of your life, not just your managerial role.

The first part of *The Secrets of Success in Management* explores what managing self means in practice by highlighting six critical areas where you need to gather insight and raise your awareness: cultivate emotional intelligence, listen actively, handle stress, give powerful presentations, network actively and write with impact.

There are, of course, many more aspects of managing self and you will discover them along the way, as your management career evolves. But for the moment, as a new or recently appointed manager, the six essentials are the ones most likely to help you survive and thrive in the early days.

Of the six, perhaps the most controversial relates to emotional intelligence (EI). Compared to the other five, which probably few informed managers would dispute, the concept of having or using EI is a relative newcomer to determining what makes a successful manager.

With some justification, critics of EI argue that it merely packages requirements that have been long-established aspects of the management scene. Whether it is new or old, EI encapsulates the idea of self-awareness and sharpening insight about oneself to interact more effectively with people.

1

Cultivate emotional intelligence

IN A TEAM MEETING, YOU NOTICE one of the normally articulate members doodling and looking glum. You could immediately call them on it but instead, you wait until after the meeting and gently pull this person aside. Tactfully, without appearing to pry, you ask, 'You seemed unusually quiet in there, and I just wondered if anything is the matter?' That is when you discover your team member's wife has breast cancer. You not only feel sad and show it, you also urge him to take the rest of the week off, to be at home and support his wife during this difficult time.

Fighting back his tears, the team member thanks you profusely and says he will do that, promising first to finish his current assignment today. Finally, you ask whether he wants the other team members to know the situation and whether he will tell them or would like you to do so.

This example of emotional intelligence (EI) in action helps explain why some managers thrive, while others mark *you need to grasp the essence of EI*

time, or fail altogether. To succeed in your new role, you need to grasp the essence of EI, and keep developing your EI throughout your career in management.

After the major impact of a pilot programme on sales, American Express trained all its financial managers and advisers in EI. PepsiCo found that if divisional leaders exhibited strengths in various EI areas, their divisions easily beat their yearly targets.

When you perceive why someone says something or behaves in a certain way, or realise when feelings in a meeting are running high and act accordingly, you show emotional intelligence. You also show it when, despite feeling angry, rather than exploding or suppressing it, you choose to redirect your anger more productively.

Soft is often the hardest

As its name implies, emotional intelligence is the ability to manage yourself and your emotions and relate to other people's emotions. These so-called 'soft skills' are in fact the hardest to learn – they do not come neatly packaged as a discrete set of techniques. Yet in explaining why people succeed in their job they matter twice as much as conventional IQ (intelligence quotient) or technical skills, argues researcher and author Daniel Goleman, who helped put EI on the map.

So, how do you make sense of emotional intelligence? How can you make sure you have your fair share of it?

- **Grow your self-awareness** – you learn to recognise your feelings as they happen and become aware how these affect you and others; you build your self-confidence.

- **Exercise self-discipline** – you discover how to express anger appropriately, coping with stress, impulses and moods; you acquire the ability to switch off and focus on the job in hand, suspending judgement and thinking before acting.

- **Use self-motivation** – in pursuit of a goal beyond money or status, you find ways to marshal emotions, improve your attention span, achieve higher levels of personal productivity, initiative, trustworthiness and self-control.

- **Show empathy** – you develop your ability to relate well to other people, and tune into the subtle signs of how they feel and respond appropriately; you become a good listener and develop organisational awareness.

- **Build relationships** – you manage emotions in others, inspire them and develop your ability to calm, cajole and handle disagreements; you build networks, rapport, leadership, influence, communication and develop others, encouraging teamwork and collaboration.

You can see people using emotional intelligence in various well-known movies. There are also famous star performers in real life who demonstrate different aspects of EI (see Table 1.1).

TABLE 1.1 *Examples of emotionally intelligent behaviours*

Emotional intelligence skill	Star performer	Movie example
Self-regard	Dalai Lama	*The Good Girl*
Emotional self-awareness	Oprah Winfrey	*The Manchurian Candidate*
Assertiveness	Dr. Martin Luther King, Jr.	*Erin Brockovich*
Independence	Mahatma Gandhi	*The Matrix, Norma Rae*
Self-actualisation	Viktor Frankl	*Whale Rider*
Empathy	Sherrol Horner Lawrence 'Chick' Patterson	*Terms of Endearment*
Social responsiblity	George Washington Carver	*Remember the Titans*
Interpersonal relationship	Jan Eller Phoebe from 'Friends'	*Something's Got to Give*
Stress tolerance	Rudolph Giuliani	*The Negotiator*
Impulse control	Anita Hill	*To Kill a Mockingbird*
Reality testing	Hans Blix	*Matchstick Men*
Flexibility	Thomas P. 'Tip' O'Neill, Jr.	*Lilies of the Field*
Problem solving	William Ulry	*GI Jane*
Optimism	Nelson Mandela	*Wizard of Oz*
Happiness	Jimmy Carter	*Love, Actually*

Source: Marcia Hughes, L. Bonita Patterson and James Bradford Terrel (2005) *Emotional Intelligence in Action*, Pfeiffer. Reproduced with permission of John Wiley & Sons, Inc.

Of course, traditional abilities still influence success. For example, intellect and cognitive skills, such as big picture thinking and long-term vision remain important. Yet when it comes to explaining excellent performance, EI consistently outclasses them.

Putting it more bluntly, plenty of highly-intelligent, smart people fail when promoted to manager. Through low emotional intelligence, they trip themselves up. For example, they prove insensitive to the feelings of others, cannot control their impatience, handle stress badly – their own and others' – are over- or underassertive, lack political awareness and so on. You can still be successful without much emotional intelligence. You just need luck, such as a booming market, weak competitors and not entirely competent senior managers.

If you are smart, you can even hide your lack of emotional intelligence, until things get tough, but then the cracks start to appear. For example, the banking industry is notorious for its poor levels of emotional intelligence and when everyone is making shed loads of money it hardly seems to matter. But once the business environment turns tough the lack of EI shows itself in knee-jerk responses such as demanding a 10 per cent across the board cut in salaries. This merely demoralises everyone and makes matters worse. Contrast this with Toyota when, during the 1997 Asian financial crisis, its Thailand operation weathered four straight years of losses with no job cuts. The order had come down from the company's president Hiroshi Okuda: 'Cut all costs, but don't touch any people.'

the higher you rise in an organisation the more emotional intelligence seems to matter

The higher you rise in an organisation the more emotional intelligence seems to matter. No wonder new or less experienced managers, who are keen to do more than just survive, ask how they can improve their EI.

Developing EI

You can deliberately grow your emotional intelligence, as decades of psychological research, training programmes and other methods show. You can learn to adjust your behaviour, moods and self-image. It is not about altering your entire personality. Rather it involves changing attitudes and habits, and acquiring knowledge and skills. Naturally, this takes time and commitment. Therefore, you need to see it as a medium-term investment, yet with significant rewards.

Not only will EI help you manage yourself, it can enable you to extract outstanding results from others. This kind of personal growth can also help you become a more fulfilled person, allowing you to guide others in developing their own emotional intelligence. As with all personal growth, it starts with your desire and intention to develop. You decide what and how you will change: in other words, who you want to be is entirely up to you.

Various well-established tests for emotional intelligence may help you assess your ability in this area. But you do not need a metric to make progress. Plenty of practical actions can enhance various aspects of your EI.

Ways to grow your EI

Make a commitment

Like a dancer who must learn a new ballet, you need to be willing to throw yourself into personal change, through constant exercise and rehearsal. For instance, what aspects of yourself do you want to retain and possibly enhance? Having a positive attitude towards personal growth explains why people persist and achieve real change.

Obtain feedback

Even the best actors need regular, honest feedback about how they come across. We are all at risk from the boiled frog syndrome in which slow changes occur, without one being entirely aware of them until too late.

Who will tell you the truth? Who, like the Roman emperors riding in triumph will whisper in your ear, 'You are only human.' That is, who might suggest changes in your behaviour? For instance, if you ask, 'Did I do that presentation well or not?' will the response be guarded or deceptively reassuring. Find ways to make it easy for people to give you honest feedback. Constantly seek out those willing to offer frank insight and suggest effective ways to try new forms of behaviour.

Dig down

Explore issues such as your personal values and your core philosophy, even when this seems far removed from the daily maelstrom of life. Work at clarifying what aspects of yourself you want to preserve, keep and relish, and those you would like to change, stimulate to grow, or adapt to your environment and situation.

Often you can do this enjoyably through development opportunities outside the organisational context. This might include external development sessions run by insightful people with no axe to grind when it comes to how you might change or grow. Various psychological tests can also help you determine or make explicit inner aspects of your real self, such as values, philosophy, traits and motives. However, tests only provide information, they are not a substitute for action.

Be inclusive

Make your self-development approach a wide-ranging one. For example, don't just focus on weaknesses such as gaps or deficiencies in your performance but give plenty of attention to your strengths too, and which ones you can enhance further. Incidentally, this is where many training programmes and organisational reviews go awry, since they start from a negative, rather than a positive position.

You may have a natural tendency to want to cut to the chase: 'Tell me where I am going wrong, so I can do something about it.' But this is not how personal growth works. Too much focus on failure or inadequacies not only batters your confidence, it can stop you seeing and valuing your genuine strengths.

Consider coaching

Good coaching can make a real contribution to enhancing your EI. It can provide a fresh perspective on how you come across and offer a reality check on where you can best concentrate your development efforts.

By learning to become a high-performance coach yourself, you will sharpen your self-awareness and build your insight into how others think, feel and act.

Allow yourself to dream

Give yourself permission to reflect on your desired future, not merely your prediction of your most likely future. This can happen through both formal and informal conversations, and even through certain kinds of tests. Maybe your organisation has no tradition of such speculative, imaginative exploration. For instance, groups may discourage such discussion, being instead highly task-focused. In this case, explore outside opportunities to free up your mind to create a mental picture of how you want the future to look. This is always the first step in making a new reality happen.

explore outside opportunities to free up your mind

Build a development plan

Growing your EI, as previously mentioned, takes time and it is easy to lose focus, either by not pursuing key issues or by becoming obsessed with just one, to the exclusion of the rest. Build yourself a personal development plan on which you can work over the next, say, 12 months. This can help prevent overusing a strength, or denying the need to adapt and change.

Set specific goals that excite or motivate you in some way. Make sure these have a coherent direction, not just a single aim. For example, merely saying you will improve your ability to listen actively (see Chapter 2) is not enough. You need to place it within a proper context, such as becoming less solution-minded or helping your people think through what they are doing, and so on.

To sum up, devise your own personal learning agenda. Others may have views on how you should change, but you should only learn what *you* want to learn.

Step beyond your comfort zone

Not everyone feels comfortable working on how to develop themselves if it means doing unusual or strange things. For example, on Maynard Leigh's personal impact courses people may find themselves standing in the spotlight of a real West End stage, explaining what inspires them. Initially participants regard such a prospect with a mixture of fear or even intense dislike. In practice, nearly everyone has a great time and makes important behavioural discoveries as a result.

So long as there seems a real prospect that it will lead to personal growth, be ready to step beyond your comfort zone and welcome such challenges.

Practise

Acting on your development plan and moving towards your personal growth goals require practise. Only through this, can you build your confidence and achieve the changes you want.

Practise may include experimenting with different ways of behaving, if necessary in a safe learning environment, such as a development workshop. These allow you to reflect on an issue, for example how to be more empathic, be more assertive or perhaps better understand relationships. Most EI growth stems from continuous learning, not a one-off activity where you tick a box and say, 'Done that, what's next?' For instance, in growing your ability to empathise with people, even if you have some successes, you still need to keep practising and learning.

Accepting that growing EI is a continuous process explains why certain managers become so successful. They continually want to learn what works, to discover more about their personal effectiveness and how best to tap into other people's motivations, needs and emotions. If necessary, seek opportunities to practise EI skills outside the organisational context. To grow your team-building capability, for instance, you may be able to create opportunities to practise these in social and community organisations, such as local clubs or professional associations.

Anticipate setbacks

If growing your EI was easy, everyone would have done it by now. As you pursue the change process, you may hit some brick walls, obstacles that slow or entirely block your progress. Consequently, make an effort to build yourself support mechanisms for these difficult times, when things do not work out as hoped or when your experiments appear unsuccessful. This might consist of adopting a mentor, scheduling discussions with selected colleagues, setting up ongoing coaching or attendance at an external event that can help put things back in perspective.

Ways to develop your EI

- ☐ *Label your feelings rather than labelling people or situations*
- ☐ *Make time to reflect on feelings, using them to identify unmet emotional needs*
- ☐ *Use your feelings to make decisions, and set and achieve goals*

- [ ] *Turn anger into productive energy, using it to energise yourself*
- [ ] *Show empathy, understanding and acceptance of other people's feelings*
- [ ] *Listen rather than advise, command, judge or lecture others*
- [ ] *Identify your fears and desires*
- [ ] *Know your core values and what really matters to you*
- [ ] *Look for the positive value of negative feelings – in yourself and others*
- [ ] *Be inclusive and let your approach to self-development be wide-ranging*
- [ ] *Consider coaching to enhance your EI*
- [ ] *Be willing to step beyond your comfort zone in how you behave and welcome such challenges*

2

Listen actively

Manager: 'Why is Peter moving to another division?'
Colleague: 'He's been unhappy for months.'
Manager: 'Why did nobody tell me?'
Colleague: 'He tried.'

That kind of conversation happens all too frequently. Tough messages often fail to surface through poor listening until too late. Make it your aim to be known as a listening manager.

Realising how poor listening could prove a costly weakness, Michael Dell, CEO and founder of Dell, the computer company, shifted its culture to be a more listening one, basing it around 360-degree feedback. Michael is famous for finding ways to listen to what customers think, rather than what Dell thinks they think.

According to a 2008 study by the London Business School, managers typically rate themselves higher than their colleagues do on most measures of performance. Some of the largest gaps appear over receptiveness to hearing about

managers do not want to hear the bad news

difficult issues. Put simply, many managers unwittingly signal that they do not want to hear the bad news. This reluctance to receive bad news is not a unique feature of the corporate world. For example, Stalin's refusal to heed reports of German troops massing at the border before the 1941 invasion of Russia is one case where the boss not only did not want to hear bad news, he even shot the messenger.

If you believe your 'open door policy' works well, check it out carefully. Your colleagues may take a different view: that it is like they are talking to a brick wall. Start by assuming you are rather less open to unwelcome messages than you think. Whether you know it or not, you may well be sending subtle signs that discourage frank input.

While most managers talk well, the best ones also tend to be excellent listeners. You have probably met people who seem to listen to what you say, without necessarily understanding or being able to respond suitably. This is the difference between listening and hearing.

Good listening is far more than remaining silent, it is a state of high alertness with several stages: receiving, understanding, remembering, evaluating and responding (see figure opposite).

According to research into listening, while we may be good at receiving we may be far less effective at the other stages:

◆ two months after listening to a talk, the average person forgets three-quarters of what was said

◆ having barely learned something, the next eight hours consist of forgetting one-third to one-half of it

◆ we think several times faster than someone talking and this partly causes the gap between listening and hearing

◆ our brains comfortably handle up to 800 words a minute while we only manage to speak at around 120 to 150 words a minute

◆ words are far less important to effective communication than other activities such as non-verbal behaviour.

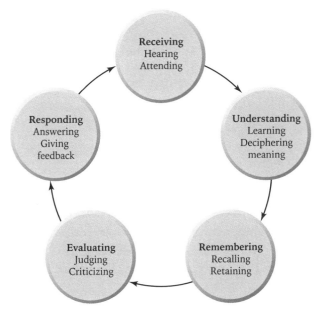

Source: From De Vito, Joseph A. *Messages: Building Interpersonal Communication Skill*, 6/e. Published by Allyn and Bacon, Boston, MA. Copyright © 2005 by Pearson Education. Reprinted by permission of the publisher.

It's situational

Your best, most active listening occurs when you are interested and have a definite purpose such as:

◆   to monitor the environment – that is listening strategically

◆   to absorb each individual's messages – discovering what they think and feel

◆   to promote communication – attending, making requests and showing understanding.

Monitor the environment

This is strategic listening. You filter out irrelevant messages to build a picture of the situation that may demand immediate action. For example, you might listen to discover:

◆   what customers say about us

◆   which channels customers use to reach us

◆   what our competitors are doing today

◆   the basis of our competitive advantage

◆   the skills or capabilities that make us unique

◆   decisions or problems that affect your own areas of responsibility.

Strategic listening keeps you in touch with current trends and sudden shifts in the organisation's environment. It is like having a radar device, constantly scanning the horizon for what is happening. It encourages you to think about the likely implications, not just for today, but for the future.

To monitor the environment keep focusing on the core issues of 'What is happening?', 'What is going on?', 'Where are events headed?'

Absorb each individual's messages

Colleague:	*'I'm a bit concerned at how this project we agreed on is going.'*
Manager:	*'It's very important you complete it on time.'*
Colleague:	*'I'm hitting some difficulties which I don't really understand.'*
Manager:	*'You're bound to meet obstacles, just keep pushing forward.'*
Colleague:	*'I'm trying, but I don't know how to deal with these issues.'*
Manager:	*'I'm sure you'll find a way through, it just takes persistence.'*
Colleague:	*'Oh, alright then.'*

This colleague feels unheard by their manager. Even though the manager seemed to be listening, the underlying message goes unheard: 'I'm in trouble and I need your help.'

In this second type of active listening, you stay alert for individual messages that help you produce results through other people. You listen to discover what people think and feel, and detect when and how best to give appropriate feedback. Recognising the value of this kind of active listening, some organisations now train their people to do it better.

you listen to discover what people think and feel

Selective listening

Faced with an individual's messages we have a natural tendency to hear what we want to hear. This explains why so many managers, like the one above, and indeed entire companies, may consistently ignore feedback that might otherwise help avoid mistakes.

Selective listening means we may misread the company's environmental impact, fail to stop faulty products or poor service, ignore impending competitor action, and underestimate employee lack of engagement and dissatisfaction.

You can spot the onset of selective listening when people start using anodyne phrases like: *'I am sure you'll find a way through.'*, *'We'll monitor the situation.'*, *'Let's keep an eye on this.'*, *'That's not really how we see it.'* These suggest avoidance and it is unlikely any action will follow.

By listening to absorb an individual's messages you:

◆ discover what is happening and the nature of current problems

◆ learn from them how problems have altered the situation

◆ obtain clues on how to avoid future problems

◆ allow people to express their feelings about their job.

At its most basic, this kind of listening reveals you as an approachable manager and builds trust between you and those who report to you. It also increases the chances that, in turn, people will listen to you.

To absorb individual messages focus on: *'What is not being said.'*, *'Other than the actual words, what else am I hearing?'*, *'What does this person feel right now?'*, *'What are the implications of this person's message?'*

Promote communication

Active listening also promotes communication by making it obvious you are paying attention. When we are intensely interested we tend to do this naturally, but not everyone does it enough. To improve your active listening to promote communication make requests, ask questions, express understanding and use non-verbal signals.

Eye contact

If you ever want to stop a salesperson from droning on, simply stay silent and resist any eye contact. Within about two minutes they will inevitably grind to a halt. Eye contact can stimulate or deter communication but positive eye contact consists of more than merely staring into someone's eyes. Holding eye contact for about 70 to 80 per cent of the time conveys interest and attention; more than this may cause people on the receiving end to feel uncomfortable or threatened.

Hunched over a PC or laptop one can easily forget all about eye contact and wonder why people find us uncommunicative. Similarly, you deter, rather than encourage communication by continually looking away from people, glancing down or over their shoulder in search of something more interesting, or flitting back and forth with your eyes as they speak.

Develop your eye contact awareness and experiment with different approaches. For example, you might hold intense eye contact while talking but show far less when listening. Or use the 'triangle' where you look at someone's eye for about five seconds, look at the other eye for five seconds and then look at the mouth for five seconds, and keep on rotating in this way. This technique, coupled with other listening skills such as nodding, occasional agreement words such as 'yes', 'uh-huh', 'mm', etc., is a great way to keep the talker talking and to show them you are interested in what they are saying.

Body language

Watch any sitcom on TV without the sound, and you soon see how body language conveys strong messages almost effortlessly. You hardly need the words to explain the humour behind the movements.

Body movement makes a big difference to how people view you as a listener.

The body cannot lie and people automatically pick up inner thoughts, feelings and attitudes from almost invisible clues. Even so, you can influence your body language to send a clear message of interest through minor gestures such as leaning towards the other person, nodding, smiling, keeping your arms open rather than folded, all suggesting that you want to hear more and are paying close attention.

Next time you talk to a colleague try staying conscious of your body language and afterwards make a list of the different movements you adopted. How many of them happened entirely spontaneously and how many did you adopt consciously?

Facial expressions

If the eyes are windows to the soul, the face is like a street poster with headlines on it. We learn in childhood to watch people's faces for clues about what they are thinking and instinctively detect gaps between the words and the actual person's meaning or intention. However, we usually give far less attention to our own facial expressions and their effect on other people. You may think you are only frowning slightly, but to those on the receiving end it may be like a red, flashing, warning light. Your smile may be a mere twitch, but to a subordinate it may seem more like a sunburst.

Facial expressions can support or undermine your active listening. Try standing in front of a mirror and convey the following through your face alone: anger, curiosity, disapproval, agreement, confusion, wonder, amusement, approval, interest, satisfaction, impatience, tiredness, dismay, encouragement, praise.

We often underrate the effect our facial expressions have on people and how they affect the appearance of genuine listening. Next time you listen to someone, try monitoring your facial expressions and see if you can detect how they influence the other person.

Use mirroring

Mirroring or reflecting back the body positions of the other person can be a powerful way to encourage communication. For example, if the other person crosses their arms you might do the same. If they place their hands in a steeple shape, you might reflect that back, mirroring their gesture.

mirroring can be a powerful way to encourage communication

Mirroring though needs care and sensitivity, not performed robotically. When you give someone your undivided attention you will tend to do it without thinking.

Rather than mirroring the other person exactly, instead try reflecting back their gestures in your own way, staying in tune with the other person and showing alignment with their gesture.

Requests

Requests based on listening are yet another way of encouraging communication. Open-ended questions, for instance, prompt people to continue talking. Pose fact-seeking questions where you ask the other person for information, while showing that you have heard what they have said so far.

People also experience your undivided attention when you start probing for clarification. In a patient, neutral way, ask the other person to be more specific:

- How is pressure on the team increasing?
- Can you give me an example?
- What do you think we can do about the situation?
- What do you need to do this?
- What happened?
- How can I help?
- How many were there?

Verbal signals

Verbal signals further oil the communication wheels and show you are paying attention. These include conversation stimulators such as saying 'mm', 'I see', 'really?' Do you usually remember to give such signals, or do you need to make a special effort to use them?

Listening is not enough

As we saw earlier, it is not enough to show you hear what the person says. People need to feel understood and ways to convey this include showing empathy, reflecting back feelings, paraphrasing, summarising and not interrupting.

Empathy

You listen with empathy by putting yourself mentally in the place of the other person. That is, you attempt to understand what they mean and what they feel. You try to see the world as they see it. When you show empathy, it builds your relationships with people.

Empathy involves your readiness to get alongside someone notionally and show you care about what they are feeling and saying. Fake empathy, though, is worse than none at all. People can quickly detect when someone is pretending to care.

Reflecting back feelings

This can be tricky territory for managers, especially some men. If you find handling feelings difficult and would prefer to avoid them you are certainly not alone, but to thrive as a manager you definitely need to become more comfortable with this aspect of the job.

A useful guideline you can adopt is:

◆ when a person talks about facts, ask about feelings

◆ when a person talks about feelings, ask about the facts.

When you notice someone's strong feeling such as anger, despair, delight or confusion, do not try to push it back down again by refusing to acknowledge what is going on. Instead, reflect back this information to the other person to show you have been listening. To reflect back what you have discovered you say things like: 'I can see you are angry about that', 'You seem to be worried about it, is that right?', 'You look really pleased about it'.

Paraphrasing

You may need to check out what you have heard and a simple way is briefly to paraphrase the conversation. By producing your own, condensed version of the other person's message, you can check on the accuracy of your understanding and seek confirmation you have it right. Part of this technique uses key word repetition where you pick out particular words or phrases to encourage the speaker to explain in more detail. When you listen carefully with the intention of paraphrasing, these key words tend to jump out at you, demanding attention.

At almost any time during the communication, you can paraphrase what someone has said and it will help show you have been giving your full attention. When you paraphrase, you add to a person's theme or argument, rather than taking it apart in a critical fashion.

Summarising

This is similar to paraphrasing except that you bring added clarity to the situation by interpreting the conversation. When you summarise you signal you have been following the communication well and it provides reassurance. Your summary should be easy to follow without excess detail, yet not ignoring crucial aspects or qualifications.

Not interrupting

Do you finish people's sentences for them, or find yourself impatient to have your turn at speaking? If so, you could be a serial interrupter. This is akin to having bad breath – probably only your best friends will let you know the truth so start asking around for feedback.

Interrupting is not always counter-productive as sometimes it can actually show enthusiasm and take the communication to another level. But generally interrupting sends a clear message that you are not listening well enough. (See also the next section.)

interrupting is not always counter-productive

Avoid being a difficult listener

Do you find it relatively easy to stay silent when with other people? It is a real strength if you feel comfortable with silence, leaving plenty of airtime for others to communicate. However, your ease with silence could also make you seem passive and a difficult listener. Equally, if you have a lot to say, silence may not exactly be your natural strength. Difficult listeners do any of the following.

◆ Give little or no feedback. This kind of static listener remains almost motionless with few facial expressions. *Try responding to specific comments with different expressions, for example, smiling, using eye contact creatively, nodding, sitting forward in response to something someone has said.*

◆ Offer monotonous feedback. You appear to be listening but your responses hardly vary, regardless of what the other person says.

Experiment with different ways of offering feedback, for example, asking questions, sharing a story, offering some new information, building on what the person has just said.

◆ Overreact. You give extreme responses to just about everything and your reaction is excessively intense, even when the other person says something low key or neutral.
Try taking notes or drawing a mind map to distract you from becoming overinvolved while still staying present.

◆ Show avoidance. You nod and offer apparent encouragement while looking around at others, but seldom at the person talking.
Try keeping your attention steadily on the other person when they are speaking and hold it there briefly, even when they stop talking.

◆ Seem preoccupied. While someone is talking or wanting attention you fiddle with papers, look distracted or multitask, perhaps using a laptop or mobile phone.
Try putting all distractions out of reach, including turning off your mobile and retain eye contact.

◆ Interrupt. This is a sure way to show lack of attention. It also conveys disrespect for the other person.
Try counting to 10 after someone has stopped speaking before responding. Also, while listening, give yourself some tasks such as trying to detect what the person might be feeling, or working out how to build on what they have said.

Do you do any of these things? If so, they could undermine you as an effective listener. If you are unsure, ask colleagues to give you feedback on how they experience you as a listener.

Ways to be an effective listener

☐ *Focus your listening by adopting a definite purpose*

☐ *Listen strategically – that is, listen for the bigger picture*

☐ *Don't merely listen, show you are paying attention*

☐ *Use and maintain eye contact, without doing it excessively*

☐ *Seek to understand both facts and feelings*

☐ *Empathy builds your relationships with people but make sure it's genuine*

☐ *Reflect back feelings – demonstrate that you have noticed them*

☐ *Use paraphrasing and summarising to convey effective listening*

☐ *Avoid being a difficult listener by offering clear feedback and not interrupting*

3

Handle stress

AFTER LOSING MILLIONS OF POUNDS, a despairing trader at *Société Générale* jumped to his death from the company headquarters. A year later, in illicit deals during 2008, Jérôme Kerviel, another trader, lost his bank not millions but billions. After the first death, you might imagine the bank's managers would start looking for abnormal behaviour on the trading floor. But apparently they missed the fact that Kerviel had turned into a virtual zombie, from losing large sums in trades.

Glued to his desk for up to 16 hours at a stretch, Kerviel held no conversations with colleagues, answering their queries only with a robotic 'yes' or 'no'. Asked to take a month's holiday he flatly refused, yet no one stopped him continuing to trade.

The essential message is to develop your awareness about stress and, when you spot it, tackle it systematically. Colleagues may feel reluctant to admit to it, preferring to hide behind the excuse of having flu, being unwell, or like Kerviel, claiming to be too busy. More than one in three young employees under 24, for example, say they will not talk openly with their managers about feeling stressed.

Managers also often neglect their own health until too late. For some, the adrenaline rush of the job can be so addictive they find it difficult to break away. For instance, nearly one-third of employees say their boss ignores workplace stress. As management science pioneer Russ Ackoff put it, working harder and harder doing 'the wrong thing righter' will not lead to success (quoted in the *Financial Times*, 17 June 2008).

Many of us actually enjoy working under pressure, and elite performers thrive on pressure – they excel when the heat is turned up. 'You can't stay at the top if you aren't comfortable in high-stress situations,' says sports psychologist and executive coach Graham Jones. But while stress can sometimes bring out the best in us, it turns nasty when it starts to undermine health and well-being.

First manage your own stress

Managing stress starts from the moment you take on a managerial role. A DDI survey in 2007, for example, found almost 60 per cent of managers see promotion as one of the most stressful events in their lives; in many cases, more than bereavement. Those most affected by this transition to anxiety are in the junior and middle ranks.

Once you can manage your own stress well, you will be better equipped to help others cope with theirs. In fact, how you handle stress may well determine whether your managerial career is a short or a long one.

Despite legal attempts to limit hours, quality of life surveys suggest nearly three out of four managers now work more than 50 hours a week. The personal and corporate cost of failing to handle stress keeps soaring. In the past, companies ignored it and seldom faced claims for damages or action over stress. Now it happens regularly, with costly litigation proving damaging to both finances and reputation.

Stress is really a stand-in for something more fundamental – the failure to organise the work environment more effectively. Once, the most painful experiences in life were bereavement, divorce and moving house. Now, for many managers, and those they manage, work itself has become the most stressful experience.

First steps

So what can you do about stress? Human beings are highly adaptable and creative. Perhaps stress is simply inevitable, to be tolerated as part of the expected price of a managerial career? By taking stress seriously, you improve your chances of both surviving and thriving as a manager. Reject macho comments from colleagues that stress is what life is all about, or 'if you can't stand the heat, get out of the kitchen.'

Showing that you care about stress demonstrates you realise it can seriously damage effectiveness and productivity. By accepting that it is your problem, you can start taking action:

◆ monitor what is happening and spot the symptoms

◆ develop remedial strategies.

Monitor and spot the symptoms

'If you cannot measure it you cannot control it' proves particularly apt in the area of stress. The more you raise your awareness of what is going on, the more insight you will be able to bring to the situation.

Consider conducting routine risk assessments to measure the current working climate. For this you can use surveys and other techniques, such as encouraging discussion with employees to identify issues and possible improvements. Would you recognise your own stress symptoms? (See the box opposite.) The Management Standards developed by the UK Health and Safety Executive (HSE) set norms for when you should seek help to tackle stress. These apply both to you and to those you manage.

One of the most obvious signs of stress comes from absence rates. CIPD Adviser Ben Willmott cites stress as being the second most common cause of absence amongst employees who take an average of 21 days to recover and return to work (*People Management*, June 2008).

It may be easier to spot the symptoms in others than in yourself and it can be difficult sometimes to realise they may indeed be a result of stress. To watch out for your own stress and tackle it systematically, review the following:

◆ *demands* – such as your workload, work patterns and the work environment

◆ *control* – the amount of say you have in how you work

◆ *support* – the extent of encouragement and resources received from the organisation, other managers and colleagues

◆ *relationships* – such as promoting positive working to avoid conflict and dealing with unacceptable behaviour

◆ *role* – making sure people understand their role within the organisation and ensuring there are no conflicting roles

◆ *change* – such as how you manage all kinds of organisational change and communicate it across the organisation.

Signs you are under stress

◆ **Physical**. Breathless; headaches; fainting spells; chest pains; sweating; nervous twitches; cramps or muscle spasms; pins and needles; high blood pressure; feeling sick or dizzy; constant tiredness; restlessness; sleeping problems; constipation or diarrhoea; craving for food; indigestion or heartburn; lack of appetite; sexual difficulties.

◆ **Feelings**. Aggressive; loss of interest in others; irritable; no interest in life; depressed; neglected; bad or ugly; there's no one to confide in; fearing diseases; fearing failure; loss of sense of humour; dreading the future.

◆ **Behaviour**. Difficulty making decisions; avoiding difficult situations; frequently crying; difficulty concentrating; nail biting; denying there's a problem; unable to show true feelings.

In ticking off your own reactions, you can get an idea of your characteristic responses to stress.

Develop remedial strategies

Being a professional dancer is one of the most stressful jobs in the world. The daily regime is gruelling. Only by strict disciplines of rigid routines, lengthy warm-ups and carefully timed breaks do the most dedicated dancers avoid injury and minimise the effects of stress. Like a dancer, unless you take control over your body and your life, you cannot expect to handle stress well. Prevention is by far the best strategy.

prevention is by far the best strategy

A core part of the strategy for handling stress is to become skilled at prioritising work, eliminating unnecessary tasks and, if necessary, obtaining help with deadlines and goals. Do this first for your own job, by negotiating upwards on what needs to change. Then help those you manage to do it. (See also Chapter 14.)

Take holidays

Take your holidays! Sounds obvious, but if you asked 10 UK workers if they use their full holiday entitlement 6 would reply that they do not. Many managers feel too pressured to enjoy their allowance. Yet what message does that send to those up and down the line?

If you cannot manage without missing your holidays, you are almost certainly not managing well in the first place. Use all your holiday entitlement, if necessary in lots of short breaks. Let people discover how much they need you! Insist that those working for you take their holidays too. Monitor holiday leave and reject arguments that they are too busy or like their work so much they can't bear to leave it.

Further elements of your systematic approach might include talk about it, get physical, laugh, obtain/provide coaching, have a healthy diet, learn relaxation and value sleep.

Talk about it

It is said that a problem shared is a problem halved. Sharing your stress levels can pass some of the strain to others who can then offer their support and encouragement to help find a solution. Members of staff, your spouse, parents or friends may all be able to help you pull through. Never be scared to ask for advice – it happens to all of us.

It can be tempting to soldier on, assuming stress must be borne as part of the job. Instead, share your problems with colleagues by being willing to talk to them about the pressure of work. However, be careful not to dump your troubles on those you supervise. They already have enough stress of their own to cope with.

Get physical

Had a good sob recently? Stress can make you want to cry and this can be a good idea, even for men! You may not want to be seen doing it at work, but there is nothing wrong with occasionally feeling tearful and letting go in a safe environment. Crying reduces tension in the body by releasing a natural hormone that makes us feel better.

Your body needs to unwind, which is why so many gyms flourish in locations where people feel under stress. But avoid driving yourself to exhaustion with a punishing schedule of physical activity. Regular exercise in which you get nicely breathless will often be enough. Try using a pedometer and see if you can manage 10,000 steps a day.

Relaxation methods can take no more than 5–10 minutes, yet make a big difference. Have a stretch, let your shoulders and arms relax into a comfortable position. Try shrugging, wriggling and shaking. They can all help reduce muscle tension.

Work systematically to ease the tension in your feet, ankles, calves, knees, thighs, chest, arms and neck. If you are sitting in a chair, or on the floor, allow yourself to feel as if the chair or the floor is supporting your whole weight; feel yourself letting go.

Laugh

Children love to laugh and on average do it around 400 times a day. By comparison, adults hardly laugh at all, only about 17 times a day. How often do you laugh?

When you feel stressed, laughter can seem unreachable. Yet it is good medicine and the health benefits range from strengthening the immune system to reducing food cravings to increasing one's pain threshold. When you laugh this produces antibodies and enhances the effectiveness of certain cells. In summary, laughing does good things to your immune system, and reduces the physical effects of stress.

laughing does good things to your immune system

If you are short of laughter now is the time to look around for ways to get your fair share of it. There are so many ways you can find laughter in life, you just have to want to do it.

Obtain/provide coaching

When you are on the lookout for signs of stress, in yourself or others, you may find it useful to use coaching to focus attention on what is going wrong. A good coach can help people recognise the different factors that may be causing stress and offer guidance on practical steps to reduce it to a level where it is positive, rather than a negative.

Since you learn what you teach others, you may also like to consider using your coaching skills to assist colleagues, including those that report to you, to handle stress. This can be a highly satisfying part of the coaching role which you can develop with off-site learning. (See Chapter 11.)

Have a healthy diet

Unless you are some kind of saint, most diets turn into eating exactly what you want to eat, but you feel the effects! The best diet is simply a good variety of foods, making sure you have a balance of protein from meat, fish, nuts or cheese, carbohydrates from bread, potatoes, pasta and rice, and fibre from cereal and wholemeal bread. Eat plenty of fresh fruit and vegetables, a minimum of five portions a day. Finally, cut down on saturated fat from dairy products, sugary foods and salt.

While you cannot eat yourself out of stress, a healthy diet can directly affect various aspects of it. For example, eating hurriedly, skipping meals or snacking inappropriately, eventually affect both bodily appearance and behaviour.

So, watch for a tendency to fill your management or team meetings with buns, biscuits and brownies. Try switching to fruit, nuts, raisins and health bars.

Learn relaxation

Every human being has the right to relax. But often people do not know how to let go without adopting other potentially stressful activities, such as sky diving, rock climbing or running marathons.

There are various, well-tried techniques known to induce relaxation and beneficially affect rates of breathing, blood pressure, muscle tension and heart rate. You can learn these and encourage your colleagues to learn them too.

Known methods for inducing a state of relaxation include meditation, yoga, autogenic training, progressive relaxation, visualisation and hypnosis. They can all teach you to stay calm and collected whatever your busy life throws at you. Though effective, they are no quick fix. You must be willing to practise the techniques regularly.

Value sleep

The busier you become, the more you need to value sleep and make sure you make enough time for it, no matter what work demands. Insufficient sleep is a sure route to stress and later ill health. Avoid work-related activity before going to bed and if you get up in the middle of the night for a toilet break, make it an unbreakable rule never to check to see what e-mails have piled up.

To sum up

The experience of managers around the world suggests that it is perfectly possible to resist dangerous levels of stress. First, be alert to its existence, in both yourself and others for whom you are responsible. Secondly, be prepared to confront stress, acknowledging it rather than allowing denial to reign. Thirdly, treat stress symptoms as a warning of something important going wrong, preventing you and others from performing at their best. Lastly, develop explicit strategies to tackle it on both a personal level and for those you manage.

If you detect yourself becoming addicted to being busy, to using work to avoid confronting your own stress, it is time to answer the final subversive question: 'Why don't I want to go home?'

Ways to manage stress

☐ *Show people you care about stress and be prepared to talk about it*

☐ *Look actively for signs of stress, rather than waiting for the consequences*

☐ *Become skilled at prioritising work and eliminating unnecessary tasks*

☐ *Use your full holiday entitlement*

☐ *Take back control of your schedule and how you tackle problems*

- ☐ *Share your stress levels with colleagues but avoid dumping them on others*
- ☐ *Take regular exercise and do not train to exhaustion*
- ☐ *Explore different ways to create relaxation and use these regularly*
- ☐ *Laughter is an excellent antidote to stress*
- ☐ *Consider using coaching to tackle stress, in yourself or those you manage*
- ☐ *Adopt a healthy diet to reduce some important aspects of stress*

4

Give powerful presentations

YOUR HEART THUMPS, your mouth is dry, you have sweaty hands, tightness in your chest, and a sick feeling in the stomach. No, it is not a heart attack, you are about to give a presentation. For some people, the prospect of presenting can be scarier than snakes, walking on fire or even death. It can upset even the sanest human being. Even so, giving powerful presentations proves crucial for almost all managers.

It helps to love presenting, though it is not essential. What counts most is finding a message with impact and being able to make your audience sit up and take notice. You can certainly learn to create and deliver powerful presentations. Which is just as well, since you will face constant demands for presentations, ranging from a team briefing to a progress report, from pitching for resources to announcing a new product or service. These requests will grow as you advance in seniority.

you can certainly learn to create and deliver powerful presentations

If your presentations regularly make an impact, this will have a ripple effect, beyond the original performance. Giving powerful presentations will raise your general confidence at communicating and influence a whole range of related areas including running meetings, making a case to senior managers, asking for a pay rise, explaining complex ideas, talking to new recruits and so on.

When is a verbal presentation needed?

◆ There is an urgently required decision

◆ You have a specific speaking engagement

◆ You want to communicate in person

◆ Your audience prefers you to be present

◆ There are too many complex ideas to rely solely on writing

◆ Your message does not need a written document

No matter how frequently you do it, each presentation demands fresh energy and a slightly different approach. So what will it take for your message to land with an impact? To achieve powerful presentations that people find memorable and influence action use the five Ps:

1   Preparation

2   Purpose

3   Presence

4   Passion

5   Personality

Preparation

In the Pixar animation film *Ratatouille*, the greatest chef in the world proclaims, 'Anyone can cook,' and even the rat hero turns into a celebrity chef! Well, anyone can present, simply start by assuming you can do it. If the thought goes through your head, 'I am not a strong presenter,' it sends a negative message to your subconscious, making it hard to be confident and effective. Good preparation therefore starts with adopting the right mental attitude.

'It always takes me several weeks to prepare a good spontaneous speech,' admitted that master of presenting, the author and lecturer Mark Twain. Improvisation works best when thoroughly underpinned by groundwork.

Having the right attitude will most likely arise from your investment in good preparation and solid practise.

Conduct research

Can you mentally picture your audience? I do not mean a sea of blank faces, but specific people. In fact can you think of an actual person? If so, this is an important first step in researching your audience. To make this even more concrete you might even prop their photograph in front of you as you prepare.

How does this person think? What do they most want to hear from you? To get inside your audience you need to start thinking like them. Experienced presenters for instance will even sit in an empty auditorium, imagining being a member of their audience.

If you cannot talk to your potential audience about the forthcoming presentation, do the next best thing and discuss it with people who know that audience person well. For example, a secretary or PA can often provide an invaluable insight as to how your target audience person thinks and responds to information.

Devise the framework

When you look through one of those observation windows at a major building site you will often see the framework for the construction that will soon follow. Without it the building will not work. Like erecting a building, your presentation needs a robust framework on which to support the material. One reliable framework to consider is *situation, complication, resolution.* This framework is like an adventure story in which you set the scene or describe the quest, reveal the obstacles and conclude with the denouement. Think Indiana Jones, Superman or Harry Potter.

Another good framework to use is the storyteller's reliable structure of beginning, middle and end. Presentations with these three elements allow the audience to follow the argument more easily. A visual storyboard can also help bring your presentation framework to life, using a mixture of words and pictures. The pictures can guide you to organise the material into a logical flow.

Whatever framework you adopt, be sure it supports your core message and supports you in making an impact.

Rehearse

With hardly a note in sight, the UK Conservative party leader David Cameron spoke for 90 minutes at the party's annual conference in 2008. People were impressed. Yet when you know what you really want to say, you instantly become less reliant on notes or reading your presentation in rote fashion.

Too busy to rehearse? It almost certainly means you are too busy to present and should not inflict yourself on an audience. Rehearsals make sure you know your core message and the key points you want to make. This discipline too often falls by the wayside when people feel under pressure or are overconfident. Yet even the most talented actors need to rehearse, so why not you too?

even the most talented actors need to rehearse

> *Ways to practise*
> ◆ Devise the presentation
> ◆ Practise in your head
> ◆ Say it out loud lots of times
> ◆ Do it in front of a mirror
> ◆ Use a video or audio recorder
> ◆ Try it out on friends and colleagues
> ◆ Rehearse it on site
> ◆ Present in front of the dog

Purpose

The death knell for most business presentations is when the audience, in effect, responds 'So what?' People soon forget your presentation unless it is a call to action, no matter how entertaining you make it.

To bring your presenting aim into sharper focus:

◆ write down your essential message, or core purpose

◆ decide what effect you want to achieve at different stages during the presentation

◆ write down exactly what you want to happen next.

So many managers fail at presenting simply because their core purpose remains vague or has too many angles. If your presentation message fits a short, easy-to-grasp sentence, the audience will probably 'receive it'. For example:

◆ 'We need a bigger IT investment and can achieve it by outsourcing.'

◆ 'My conference talk will encourage new clients to make contact.'

◆ 'We need major energy savings and I suggest ways to do this.'

◆ 'After meeting me, you will hire me as your key account manager.'

People will leave inspired and wanting to learn more.

Having decided on your overall purpose or the effect you want to achieve, you next need to decide on the more detailed effects you need to achieve moment-to-moment. For example, at different stages of your delivery you may want to:

- challenge

- gain agreement

- provoke

- amuse

- puzzle, or

- question.

As you develop your presentation, if you feel unsure about why you are including some fact, a story, a visual, an argument, even a sentence, ask yourself:

> *'Why am I telling them this now in the presentation? What effect or result am I trying to achieve at this moment?'*

Follow-through

After the presentation what do you want to happen next? This is your follow-through purpose. Audiences need clear guidance about what you expect of them. For example, if you want extra resources, explain this at the start *and* at the end of the presentation. In effect, you say, 'This is what my presentation will be about,' and then, 'This is what my presentation was about.'

Presence

To create a relationship with your audience you need to be fully present. This is not a mysterious magic woven only by great orators or actors. It is simply being fully there, alive, energised and alert while centre stage. More precisely, it happens when you feel attuned to everything happening in the moment. This heightened awareness makes people more receptive to your message. The highway code of presenting is one of the best ways of becoming present, and is used by countless experienced performers:

Stop! Breathe, Look, Listen.

Do these four actions before your actual presentation starts, and before you even utter a word. Experienced presenters never rush this stage, often relishing the opportunity of prolonging it.

Stop! means you literally pause and breathe, taking stock of the moment. It can be exciting, risky yet ultimately rewarding. You are, in effect, arriving and letting the audience arrive too. It allows everyone to settle down and adjust to being there. Savour the moment.

Effective breathing is no great secret. It is how great performers calm themselves and reinforce their presence. Taking a few steady, deep breaths before talking can transform how the sound comes from your mouth and helps you focus. After several steady, deep breaths, you should start experiencing a sense of calm and peace.

effective breathing is no great secret

The next part of our highway code directs you towards your surroundings. Looking around carefully, you make visual and mental contact with your audience. Pick out and make eye contact with one or two people. These may be people you know, or who you can feel comfortable with. Turn your head, use your eyes, watch for signs the audience is ready to hear you speak.

In the listening part of the highway code you absorb all the sounds around you, using it to detect further clues about what the audience might be feeling and hearing. Sometimes this reveals shuffling feet, rustling papers, tapping keyboards, murmured conversation, all signs people are not yet ready for you to perform. Listen and wait for that unmistakeable silence that says 'go ahead now'.

Connect

Powerful presentations connect with the audience at a visceral, not just a cerebral, level. A presentation that truly connects makes people tingle, smile, frown or respond in some way that goes beyond mental appreciation.

Many good speakers often achieve this connection through telling stories, pacing their speeches to hold people's attention. Others connect visually with a vivid film clip or a killer slide that conveys an idea in a compelling way. Audiences hunger for a connection with presenters.

Through exposure to television and other visual media, audiences expect intimacy, not grand gestures and sweeping phrases traditionally associated with public speaking. Instead, they want the feeling of physical closeness – spatial and emotional.

Passion

If there is no passion, you may as well just e-mail a report. Audiences expect to see your passion. Passion can transform an otherwise boring performance into one that moves, persuades, entertains and excites. Passion touches people. If you dislike the whole idea of presenting with passion, think instead of doing it with a strong commitment. Make this pervade your performance, filling it with energy and enthusiasm. When you convey what you truly care about it makes you come across as authentic – the real you.

Never believe the person who tells you the audience does not want an emotional involvement. You will profoundly misunderstand your audience if you assume they are all cerebral, rational beings cooly weighing the contents of your presentation.

In our regular work helping people to improve their presenting, they often say they are unsure about what moves them or they feel out of touch with their passion. The trouble is, audiences soon notice an absence of passion or commitment behind the message. Finding your passion for each presentation is therefore an important part of giving a good performance. To get in touch with your passion, try writing down the answers to these three questions:

1   What really matters to me about my core message?
2   What really excites me about giving this presentation?
3   After presenting, what do I most want the audience to do next?

Passion closely connects to energy. When you express strong feelings, you radiate energy and this is a gift to your audience. When people see you energised it's like charging their batteries too, they begin to feel energised themselves.

Personality

'You mean I just have to be me?' The answer is absolutely! So, what makes you special, different, interesting, attractive?

Whatever the answer, it is enough to make an impact. If you are unsure how to use your personality, start with making a list of the most important qualities you possess. Use single words, like integrity, humour, intelligence, determination, thorough, tolerant, inquisitive and reliable. Once you have your list, invite a few people you know and trust to describe you, also using single words. How does your list compare with theirs? Alternatively, try writing a description of yourself, as if you were a reporter doing a profile for a newspaper. After the interview, what would the profile say? How would it read?

Sometimes, you may need to use only part of your personality in a presenting situation. For example, when announcing the closure of a factory or the cancellation of a project, this is no time for your frivolous side to run riot.

you may need to use only part of your personality

Do you know what is it about you as a person that works well when you communicate? Do people immediately assume you are serious, jokey, in a hurry, or thoughtful? Unravelling how others see you, may allow you sometimes to do the reverse of what they expect, without worrying that you will go too far. For example, if people generally view you as amusing and a bit cheeky, then sometimes give yourself permission to be serious and choose not to be what people expect.

The truth about visuals

An engineer from Rolls Royce returned from a visit to Japan and called his team together. Placing a Japanese camera on the table he invited them to say how much it would cost for Rolls Royce to make it. Their estimates far exceeded the actual cost. In this way he rammed home his message that the team needed to rethink its approach to cost control. The engineer could have used a slide presentation, but instead made the message concrete for his audience.

No business meeting seems complete without a deadening slide show of some kind – often called death by PowerPoint. This technology becomes boringly repetitive, with a dominance of bullet points over visuals. Make sure your visuals have impact, for example, words are not visuals, nor are bullet points.

Slides also encourage speakers to keep looking at the screen, rather than the audience, using it as notes for their presentation. PowerPoint does to the brain what boiling does to vegetables and in roughly the same way. People come to hear and see you, not watch slides and animations.

Ways to be a powerful presenter

☐ *Use the five Ps: Preparation, Purpose, Presence, Passion and Personality*

☐ *Research your audience, even when you think you know them already*

☐ *Rehearse enough so you can manage without detailed notes*

☐ *Reduce the purpose of your presentation to a single headline statement*

☐ *Express the purpose of the presentation in terms
of action*

☐ *Use the highway code of presenting: Stop! Breathe, Look,
Listen*

☐ *Connect with your audience via stories, visuals and
other means*

☐ *Audiences expect to see your passion – show them!*

☐ *Use your whole personality, people want to see the real you
in action*

☐ *Avoid death by PowerPoint – it's you they want to see not
bullet points*

5

Network actively

HOW DID BILL GATES GET SO LUCKY? Why did his obscure, start-up computer company receive a totally unexpected call from Big Blue, the largest computer company on the planet? It all started with his mum. As a tireless networker, she was friends with the man who ran IBM. She told him about her son's new computer venture and that led to a crucial, once-in-a-lifetime phone call. The rest you probably know.

Reject the idea that networking is blatant self-promotion or looks bad. Networks deliver unique benefits to you including private information, access to diverse skills and power. Successful managers build networking into their way of doing business. Not everybody relishes networking though. Building a fabric of personal contacts that *networks deliver unique benefits to you* provides support, feedback, insight, resources and information seems entirely sensible. Yet, as researchers found, it is one of the most dreaded developmental challenges.

Constant attention

One reason for this dread is that a network only becomes worthwhile if you give it constant attention. It demands a readiness to contribute when you cannot be sure you will receive a full return on your investment.

Take Nick Hine, Senior Partner in the UK law firm Thomas Eggar. He constantly feeds his numerous contacts with information, leads and opportunities to network. You never quite know whom you will encounter at one of the many events he hosts during the year. When, unexpectedly, you receive a note from Nick that he has given your name to a possible useful contact he clearly does not expect any personal payoff, beyond a prompt thank you note. Nor is it surprising that he can instantly point you in the right direction as to who to talk to about an issue, whether it is legal or something else. In fact, you can usually tell a great networker like Nick immediately. Ask them a question and they instantly know someone, who knows someone who might know the answer.

Research shows that people who contribute most to an organisation tend to be those like Nick, with a cultivated network of contacts involved in professional and community activities. Networking is part of Nick's way of managing and there is no best time to do it, he simply makes it part of his daily life. It will mainly involve direct, one-to-one interactions on the phone, formal and informal meetings, e-mail and other methods of communication. It could even mean nurturing computer-based contacts, via networking sites.

Using social sites

Once, social networking meant going to the pub for an evening. Now it could also involve hours at a monitor. It may not always be obvious how social technology-based networking can support you as a manager. For example, many of those involved will be communicating with people already in their extended social network. They are not necessarily networking at all, or looking to meet new people. Such networks can be good though for keeping you in touch with people you value.

Social networks may prove of practical management use if you need to:

◆ assess a new pool of candidates for the organisation

◆ contact people you know and trust in business (e.g. via LinkedIn)

◆ learn from subject matter experts who share and discuss areas of mutual interest (e.g. through Webinars)

◆ find opportunities to encourage and promote employee involvement and engagement (e.g. through intranets and associated wikis, and web logs).

Despite the fast changes made by the social networking revolution, the basic principles of successful networking remain unchanged. You can only expect to build and nurture contacts if there is both give and take, not just take. Worthwhile networking relies on a shared willingness to do the unasked, to help when you do not have to, to give when there is apparently not much in it for you.

Talk to most effective managers and you will almost certainly find they continuously work to build contacts in other departments or elsewhere. They have long ago discovered that seniority alone does not guarantee the help they need: it takes a network of personal relationships. The critical point about networking of any kind is that it is personal. It involves you relating to other individuals, rather than an institution, often bypassing the hierarchy.

If you work in an organisation that relies on projects or temporary teams, you will need an anchor as you move from one group to another. Networks can provide this stability.

Think of your networks as a series of virtual teams to which you belong. You may never physically all meet together, yet the connections amount to a group with a stake in helping each other, whenever possible.

Making it happen

Like planting seeds in the garden, you grow strong relationships gradually. First you till the soil, plant the seeds, water, fertilise and prune where necessary. The garden grows and blossoms, then you harvest. Relationships are similar. You need to prepare yourself to become part of the network by knowing your values, having integrity and honesty, and the right tools and skills to nurture the relationships over time.

Because relationships lie at the heart of networking, there are few short cuts. It takes time to get to know people, and for them to know you. You learn each other's strengths and weaknesses, quirks, dreams and vulnerabilities. You can make contacts quickly, but meaningful relationships take longer.

it takes time to get to know people

The top 10 essentials

1 **Listen effectively** (see Chapter 2) to learn about the other person. Discover their desires, hopes and dreams. You cannot do this by constantly talking about yourself. Leave out 'me' and 'mine' from the conversation and concentrate on 'you' and 'yours'.

2 **Be trustworthy**. That is, act ethically and above reproach. Build trust by being reliable (see below) and authentic, willing to admit mistakes and confront wrong actions in others.

3 **Demonstrate reliability**. Make good on your promises and promptly. Stick with the approach of underpromise and overdeliver.

4 **Value diversity**. Recognise people have different styles, tastes and preferences. You may disagree on minor items, yet maintain a close, healthy relationship based on compatible values.

5 **Become at ease in groups**. Practise until you feel comfortable breaking into groups of all kinds. Most people are just as scared as you are and only need a little general comment to start talking.

6 **Offer care**. Show interest in people's achievements, their problems and their life.

7 **Ask for help**. Seek assistance with difficult goals or tasks. Avoid being a loner trying to do it all by yourself. Recognise you almost certainly perform best when you draw on a wide range of talents.

8 **Introduce yourself**. Be direct, open and welcoming when meeting new people. Readily explain who you are and what you stand for.

9 **Persist**. Be constant and relentless in your networking and relationship building, overriding obstacles of time and place. Develop tenaciously your network, and use multiple channels to reinforce your objective.

10 **Give feedback**. Provide information about what you did about other networkers' suggestions, introductions and offers of help or supply of material. Use feedback to build the quality and depth of the relationship.

Get a strategy

Develop a deliberate plan to understand your potential network and identify how you are going to build and nourish it. Like any major task, it needs a plan of action.

◆ Draw a network map of all your contacts. (See also Chapter 20.)

◆ Each time you have a major task review carefully who might assist you.

◆ Commit to making notes or records about every person who could be a future key contact. Start identifying how mutual help might be offered.

◆ Make relationship building one of your managerial priorities and devote meaningful time to pursuing it.

◆ Find ways to stay alert to new opportunities for relationship building.

◆ Break major projects into tasks that only you can do, and ones where other people's help would be more appropriate.

Get organised

Networking tests your organisation skills. For example, you will need to develop a reliable way to manage the information gathered about people and avoid wasted follow-up effort. There are plenty of technological fixes for maintaining a list of contacts, ranging from the 'little black book', MS Office, sophisticated relational databases and, of course, networking sites. Yet all rely on your commitment to keeping them up to date, weeding your 'garden' so the strongest plants keep growing.

Can you quickly find the names, addresses and phone numbers of all your contacts? What do you do with the business cards you acquire? Do you order and systematically file them where you can readily find them again, such as recording them in your electronic contact list?

New contacts quickly fade without an effort to reinforce the relationship early on and reasonably often. Do you have a proper follow-up system for when you meet interesting new contacts to remind you to send notes, letters, e-mails and so on?

Be people-minded

For some managers the most challenging part of networking is being people-minded, for example feeling at ease in social situations, and being happy to use formal and informal meetings to keep their networks fresh and alive. In social situations, your ability to circulate easily is another area you may need to enhance in some way: for example, the skill to turn small talk into big business.

Ways to improve your effectiveness in this area include:

◆ greeting people with a warm smile and a firm handshake

◆ taking the initiative in conversations by asking people about themselves

◆ establishing good eye contact

◆ introducing yourself and using open-ended questions that start with how, when, where or who

◆ using small talk as an ice breaker and not despising it by plunging straight into talking business.

If you feel you need to strengthen your ability or confidence in these areas then do it in stages. Pick one issue and start exploring ways to alter your approach: for example, staying alert to how you greet people and experimenting with new ways of doing this.

It is said that you only need six people to be able to reach absolutely anyone, anywhere in the world. That is, someone you know will know someone, who knows someone who.... Scientific studies have shown that this principle, called Six Degrees of Separation holds for almost any contact one wants to make. Networking is the ultimate six degrees tool, and the more people in your network the greater the chances you can reach the person you most need with the minimum number of steps.

networking is the ultimate six degrees tool

Work the room

Breaking into a group of strangers can be one of the most challenging situations for even experienced networkers. So how *do* you interrupt a group without causing offence? The secret comes down to careful observation and some basic techniques for entering a conversation. Start by getting comfortable standing on your own, so you do not feel rushed to join any group. Focus on what is happening around you, rather than what is happening inside you, the doubts and fears about the situation.

After selecting the group you want to join, check on the intensity of the ongoing conversation. Do people seem locked into each other with intense eye contact and positive body language? If so, step away from their immediate vision. Wait at a distance and watch for the intensity of the conversation to change, and then walk into the group. Listen to whoever is speaking and do not try to change the tone, pace or steal the conversation away from someone else. Only offer to shake hands if the conversation turns to you and people are keen to find out who you are.

Once the conversation changes to bring you into the group, introduce yourself and, if appropriate, shake hands. If you have something important to say, now is the time to do it. If you only want to meet a particular person say so: for example, 'I've been keen to meet you for ages, but can see you're busy right now. Could we please exchange business cards, and I will call you next week for a quick chat?'

The magic is in the conversation, asking questions and thinking more about others than yourself. As a manager, you may often find yourself the 'star turn' in a work setting and it is important not to let this go to your head. Once you allow all the attention to focus on you, while it may do wonders for your ego, it will virtually end all chances of networking and building your vital contacts.

Watching a skilled networker can be confusing – they do not seem to be doing much, yet many people keep talking to them. They move around with ease and seldom become trapped in fruitless conversations where they cannot escape without appearing to be rude. These successful networkers are usually excellent observers and listeners. They revel in other people talking, rather than talking themselves, yet they converse easily and are constantly curious. At the heart of this kind of relationship building, are alertness, observation and a readiness to move on without rushing.

As you network, many people will offer you information, opportunities and valuable contacts. Make a written note of the favours people have done for you and write each one a short thank you of some kind. People feel naturally drawn to someone who readily shows appreciation for past help.

look for opportunities to create a mutual relationship

Networking is not about selling something to someone who does not want it. Instead, you look for opportunities to create a mutual relationship where you give as much as you take. Remind yourself that your focus is on the relationship, not on immediate results.

The best management networkers build the activity into their daily life, continually adding value to relationships.

They act as connectors, recommenders and allies who look out for you.

Ways to network actively

☐ *Make networking a constant part of your daily life, not a sporadic effort*

☐ *Ensure you build in plenty of give, not just take*

☐ *Think of your networks as a series of virtual teams to which you belong*

☐ *Know your values*

☐ *Develop the tools and skills to nurture relationships*

☐ *Develop a plan to understand your network and how you will build and nourish it*

☐ *Be trustworthy; that is act ethically and above reproach*

☐ *Demonstrate reliability*

☐ *Recognise people can have different styles, tastes and preferences*

☐ *Become comfortable joining and participating in groups of all kinds*

☐ *Show interest in people's achievements, their problems and their life*

☐ *Seek assistance with difficult goals or tasks*

☐ *When meeting new people be direct, open and welcoming, readily explaining who you are and what you stand for*

☐ *Be tenacious in developing your network*

☐ *Offer feedback to your contacts to build the quality and depth of the relationship*

☐ *Note the favours people do for you and show your appreciation*

6

Write with impact

'NO HARD HAT, NO WORK.' Visit any large UK building site and you will probably spot a large notice along these lines. Yet it might equally read: 'Any employee entering this building site is at risk of injury or death, wearing a hard hat is a condition of employment and anyone not wearing one will be liable to instant dismissal.' Which version would immediately grab your attention, the five-word version or the other?

The need to write with impact keeps growing in importance. This is despite the emphasis driven by various communications technologies on speed at the expense of quality. Most organisations expect their managers to become adept at writing. This means the ability to gain attention, whether through reports, concise feedback or incisive e-mails.

On a purely technical level, writing with impact involves avoiding common written mistakes. The most frequent mistakes are missing words and punctuation (see figure overleaf).

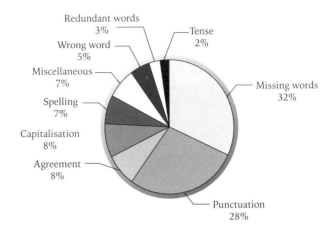

Source: White Smoke Software, reproduced with permission.

However, some of these requirements seem to be fraying at the edges. There is now less emphasis, for instance, on perfect spelling, punctuation, grammar or even writing complete sentences. You can send a grammatically correct note to everyone in your team, for example, yet why would anyone bother reading it? It takes more than good grammar or status to ensure written impact.

Know your audience

Agonising over what to write or how to write it mainly stems from not knowing your audience well enough. Getting inside the head of your audience may sound impossible, yet it is the first principle of high-impact writing.

For example, do you know what would grab your audience's attention and why? Can you anticipate their objections or resistance to your message? What priorities do your audience have and what needs will your writing meet? Answering such questions is part of the research side of producing writing with impact.

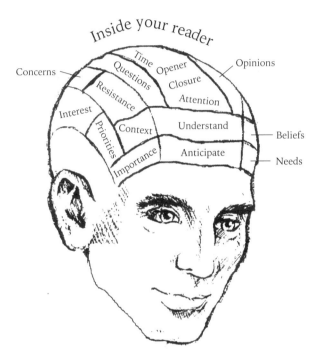

Write for a person

Start by writing for one specific person, rather than a group of people, even when they will ultimately also be the audience. By choosing a specific person to be your audience, you can keep this person constantly in mind. You can almost 'talk' to them through your writing. You might even consider putting a photograph of them in front of you while writing, in a similar way to that when you are presenting (see Chapter 4).

The person you write for almost certainly does not just want information, even if that appeared in the original brief. For your writing to achieve impact, it also needs to add value. That means first attracting the recipient's attention and then delivering messages they find useful. You cannot take their attention for granted and many will be as time-pressurised as you are.

Use the right order

To ensure you have arrived at a clear purpose, first of all create a single short headline of no more than half a dozen words to sum up what you want to say.

Two other solid ground rules affecting the impact of writing are:

1   Place the most important message at the start, not in the middle or towards the end. Headlines grab attention. Show five people an advertisement and only one will read beyond the headline. Place your main message in the headline and confirm it in the opening paragraph.

2   Put background information first and new information later. This helps people relate to what they already know.

Be concrete

Stick to concrete rather than abstract words and sentences. This will avoid forcing your reader to unravel your meaning. For example:

Abstract: *'This month's sales figures have proved less satisfactory than we originally hoped.'*

Concrete:	*'We have disappointing sales figures this month.'*

Use the unexpected

You will also strengthen your writing if you can tell people something they did not already know. Reports that regurgitate old news, old information or well-known current facts, turn readers off. It may work in purely technical writing to explain laboriously the background to an issue but this becomes a death wish when used for management writing.

Use the unexpected to hold people's attention. Pose a question, reveal a gap, present a problem and then take the reader through to a satisfactory ending, such as proposals for action. Using the unexpected can be as simple as asking your reader if they know what current competitors are up to and then telling them the answer. It might be describing an emerging gap between the agreed plan and what is happening on the ground.

use the unexpected to hold people's attention

Use the unexpected to grab your reader's attention and then do not let go. Tell the story behind it and lead on to answers or suggestions, advocate a course of action or present a conclusion.

Use the active

It is worth getting to grips with active versus passive writing. Active writing comes across as more direct and forceful.

This is a tricky area since you must put the subject of the sentence first, rather than at the end. It usually uses fewer words.

Active writing conveys energy, for example:

Passive: *'The team morale was badly affected by the product recall.'*

Active: *'The product recall badly affected team morale.'*

Passive: *'As a direct consequence of the economic downturn it will be necessary to take action.'*

Active: *'We need to take action over the economic downturn.'*

Develop your style

The demand for high impact writing in organisations can be particularly challenging to new managers and recent graduates perhaps more used to writing college essays or purely technical reports.

Writing with impact in organisations demands both clarity and brevity. To achieve this you may need to develop a more robust writing style. For example, if your sentences expand beyond 15–20 words you risk losing your reader.

Similarly, avoid mind-numbingly lengthy paragraphs. Impactful management writing mainly depends on short paragraphs of around four or five lines that hold onto your reader by keeping the number of key points to a minimum.

In the age of text messaging and terse e-mails, the long paragraph can be the kiss of death for readability and impact.

Hints on how to rite good

◆ Avoid clichés like the plague; they're old hat.

◆ Spare the quotations. 'Tell me what you know' demanded a famous writer.

◆ It behoves you to avoid archaic expressions.

◆ Exaggeration is a billion times worse than understatement.

◆ The passive voice should be avoided – instead use the active.

◆ Who needs rhetorical questions?

◆ Avoid commas, that, are not, necessary.

◆ Be more or less specific.

◆ Use your spell checkker to avoid mispelings and typo errers.

◆ Don't never use no double negatives.

◆ Always avoid alliteration.

◆ Don't repeat yourself, or say again what you have already said.

◆ Never use a big word when a diminutive would suffice.

◆ Poofread to see if it is at all possible to cut out any of the excess words you use.

Is your report necessary?

Beware the black hole! After labouring over a report, perhaps for days or weeks, at last it is printed and distributed. To your intense disappointment, it gains no noticeable response. When this happens, you have probably fallen victim to the black hole of the unwanted report.

Most managers receive a steady request for written reports. Whether as bound tomes or lengthy e-mail replies, organisations effortlessly absorb information-rich missives. This does not mean they make any difference. Rather than rush to produce a written response, first explore what seems to lie behind the request. A verbal report, supported by a single-page summary, will often prove more effective and perfectly acceptable. For example, Toyota insists all presentations have a one-page summary setting out background information, objectives, analysis, action plans and expected results.

By uncovering the reason behind the request you can then decide how best to write the material. Judicious digging may also reveal that the true reason for the request differs significantly from the one you started with.

Use a strategic context

Whenever possible, place your material within a strategic context. This means relating it to what the organisation wants to achieve – its strategic intent. For example, frame your report within the organisation's broad aims, plans, aspirations and vision for its future. At your particular management level, you may not know either the strategic context or the nature of existing plans. Well, now is the time to find out. Simply asking the questions will tend to raise your personal profile and word soon gets around.

New or inexperienced managers tend to write overlong reports weighed down with excessive detail. Equally, the novice's report may be over concise, leaving the reader frustrated at insufficient evidence and uncertain about the proposed next actions and reasons for these.

Too short or too long, how do you pitch it just right? It all comes down to clarity about what you want to achieve. Someone asking you the time does not want to know how to build a watch. Organisational reports are not essays but action-focused text. No matter how complicated an issue it can usually be confined to one or two pages.

how do you pitch it just right?

Your written reports need to cover the three simple stages of writing with impact.

◆ **Prepare** is about indentifying the issues, clarifying terms of reference, gathering the information and analysis. This may feel like college essay writing but, as mentioned, it is far more action focused and less discursive or abstract. You also need enough time to prepare, rather than pushing ahead with the writing. Be willing to negotiate around deadlines and the degree of urgency.

◆ **Produce** involves structuring your report with a logical framework, into which you fit the material. Tell people the unexpected, not what they already know, and provide an action focus with an emphasis on quickly conveying the key points in an easy-to-follow sequence. This stage also includes writing, testing, revising, editing and above all summarising.

◆ **Persist** is the final stage, and usually the most neglected. Never willingly drop your report into a black hole by delivering it to your audience and merely hoping for the best.

How to avoid writer's block and other tips

If writing a report fills you with dread, you are certainly not alone. It can feel daunting to commit ideas, suggestions and conclusions to the written word. A tip for this early stage of the activity is:

> *Don't get it right, get it written, then get it right.*

Rather than agonising over whether your report immediately works, has impact or offers the unexpected, the first time around give yourself permission to splurge out on anything and everything. Waste no time on grammar, logic or even the full content. Just make a start. You will soon generate more than enough material.

The real work begins in reordering material, eliminating unnecessary information (pruning), filling in gaps, and identifying the core message along with suggestions for action.

Use a powerful heading

Choose a snappy heading to grab your reader, one that encapsulates your entire message. You are not writing for an academic journal but to achieve action.

Provide a summary

A good summary leaves your reader feeling they have mastered the material so far. If you cannot sum up your report in a couple of paragraphs it is almost certainly too long or complicated for most management purposes.

Production

Production and distribution of the report matter and this includes filtering out all signs of hurry, inattention to detail or slapdash appearance.

The people who need the report may be different to those who originally requested it. In displaying it consider how best to attract your potential readers. For example, be wary of using lots of UPPER CASE to draw attention to its importance. PEOPLE SOON GET FED UP WITH LOTS OF CAPITALS. Also, avoid adding a pleading covering note such as 'Please read this, it is very important.' As opposed to what? Eat it or use it for origami?

Finally, be selective when distributing your report. These days the e-mail 'Select All' button can be a deadly device for ensuring your material dies a natural and wasteful death. If those on the receiving end feel just one of a crowd, many may delete the e-mail without even reading it!

be selective when distributing your report

Make each recipient of your report feel special by how you distribute it. For example, in some cases a personal delivery of the physical report along with a 30-second explanation can really help to ensure it gains more than a cursory glance.

The three-thirds guidelines

You may find it helpful to adopt the three-thirds guidelines for writing with impact:

◆ spend one-third of your time and energy on researching and preparation

- spend one-third of your time and energy on writing
- spend one-third of your time and energy on persistent follow-up.

For many people, writing proves the easy part. Presenting it and ensuring follow-through action often proves much harder. Persistence in follow-through ensures your writing labours appear on suitable agendas and achieve quality time for consideration.

The chore of writing a management report can feel so demanding that some people have no energy left for follow-through. Having finished it, they fire it off with relief, then sit back and wait for something to happen.

No management report is truly effective without persistent follow-through. This applies even to ones that gain widespread approval. Reserve enough energy to persist with the final stage. Arrange meetings to discuss it, demand action, invite feedback on what happened since you delivered it, and ask questions about what action needs to occur next and so on. You may even find it useful to issue a short follow-up report.

Persistent follow-through builds your reputation for thoroughness. Once people realise you tackle requests in depth and with persistence, many potential requests may disappear in favour of a shorter verbal presentation.

Make it persuasive

If it is worth putting in writing, it is worth ensuring your writing is persuasive with a focus on action. There is more on persuasion in Chapter 20. Being action-minded is a way of life and needs to pervade your management style and especially your reports.

Ways to write with impact

☐ *Explore what seems to lie behind the request for a written report*

☐ *Pay close attention to how people will receive your written messages*

☐ *Don't get it right, get it written, then get it right*

☐ *Make your written communications add value, not just distribute information*

☐ *Place your most important message at the start*

☐ *Stick to concrete rather than abstract words and sentences*

☐ *Use active rather than passive forms of sentence construction*

☐ *Provide a strategic context for your reports*

☐ *Written reports usually need three simple stages: prepare, produce, persist*

☐ *Use a powerful heading to grab your reader and encapsulate your message*

☐ *Provide an easy-to-read summary*

☐ *Make each report recipient feel special by the distribution method used*

☐ *Reserve enough energy after writing to ensure you can follow-through*

☐ *Be action focused, offering ways forward and solutions*

PART 2

Manage others

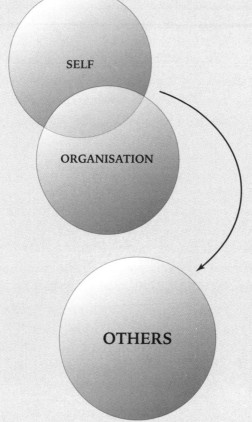

Others

- ◆ Show leadership
- ◆ Manage your team
- ◆ Manage your boss
- ◆ Review performance
- ◆ Coach for results
- ◆ Negotiate successfully
- ◆ Manage problem people

Managing others requires you to hone your awareness of what they need to be effective, applying your insight to helping them perform at their best, unlocking their potential.

These seven aspects of being a manager focus on key areas where newcomers often struggle to make headway: show leadership; manage your team; manage your boss; review performance; coach for results; negotiate successfully; and deal with problem people.

You could argue this part encompasses everything management is all about and into which all the rest should fit. Though a legitimate view, if you are starting on the management road the above grouping can prove helpful in nailing down the essentials.

Countless books, workshops, seminars and conferences revolve around these seven processes. Some, like performance reviews, generate strong feelings, since so few managers seem to relish doing them. Yet one can hardly conceive of a successful manager who has not to some extent mastered the seven processes described here.

A theme running through this part on managing others is making sure people feel aligned to the corporate strategy and feel fully engaged. The Global Workforce study by Towers Perrin in 2007 brought into sharp focus the extraordinary underused potential of so many people at work. Its survey of 90,000 people across 18 countries found most people at work withhold their full range of abilities. In the UK, for example, a minuscule 14 per cent of employees feel fully engaged with their work and therefore are performing to their maximum. That leaves a huge 86 per cent of people who could perform better.

When engagement goes missing in action, ambitious managers are rightly concerned. In terms of profits, companies with highly-engaged staff significantly outperform those with less-engaged staff by a wide margin.

An engaged employee is most likely to say:

- ◆ 'I believe rewards are fairly distributed.'
- ◆ 'I feel respected and listened to.'
- ◆ 'The management here is visible and accessible.'
- ◆ 'They support new ideas here.'
- ◆ 'I am improving my skills.'
- ◆ 'I believe my organisation has a sincere interest in supporting me.'

If you can get your people saying these kinds of things, and initially focus on the seven key management processes of this part, you will almost certainly survive and thrive in your new role.

7

Show leadership

BRIAN PICKED UP THE PHONE to hear his boss asking to see him right away. Slightly anxious about this unexpected summons, he ran down the corridor and was in the other office within half a minute. As usual, his boss had that permanently serious look on his much-lined face.

'Brian, thanks for coming so promptly. Why I called you is quite simple. I want your resignation as a manager.' Brian sat up shocked, and the colour drained from his cheeks. 'What, why? What's gone wrong?'

'Nothing,' replied his manager, obviously relishing the drama, 'I want your resignation as a manager because I need you to start acting as a leader.' The rest of the meeting went by in a blur. But Brian never forgot the day he stopped thinking like a manager and began acting like a leader.

Is there a difference between being a leader and being a manager? Having signed up to be a manager, you may feel the job is already large enough, without also worrying about being a leader. Many organisations, though, now expect managers to *once, managing versus leading was simple*

show leadership. Once, managing versus leading was simple. Managers made things happen efficiently, while leaders concentrated on doing what is right, focusing on values, direction and inspiring people. This neat distinction never really made sense, and proves increasingly unhelpful. So how do you show leadership and is it something you can learn?

According to mythology, a powerful charisma underpins leadership. Yet those running successful, long-lasting organisations prove to be different from the high-profile, larger-than-life personality conventionally associated with top leaders. In fact, the most outstanding ones are a study in duality, modest and wilful, humble and fearless. That could equally describe many managers, who never perhaps consider themselves as leaders in the formal sense.

To show leadership, therefore, it is not necessary to brim with charisma or cause entire rooms to fall silent when you enter. A seven-year study of middle managers (**www.bulletpoint.com**) uncovered the three big steps to taking a lead without being a leader: position, share and influence.

1   **Position to lead**: create more time for strategy and to obtain information and opinion from beyond the organisation; reorganise the team so you become less central to its everyday tasks.

2   **Share information**: pass on what you learn, especially from customers and other external partners; help reorientate people around goals aligned to your own.

3   **Influence not order:** continue to work *with* colleagues, without lecturing them; view the current situation from their perspective; look for ways to modify and simplify procedures, rather than replacing them or adding complex new tasks onto them.

Beyond these basics, you also show leadership when you:

◆   select what needs to be done

◆   think about the future and what is right for the organisation

◆   develop action plans

◆   take responsibility for decisions

◆   initiate communication

◆   focus on opportunities rather than problems

◆   run productive meetings

◆   think and say 'we' rather than 'I'

◆   show you care about your people so they develop trust in you.

Running like a thread through all these actions are two strands that allow you to show leadership while still nominally being a manager: you need to be proactive and be authentic. Being proactive means you take initiatives, set examples, volunteer for assignments and make things happen. Each of these can help demonstrate your leadership in highly practical and often visible ways. Being authentic is simply being yourself, doing what you say you will do, and showing integrity.

Select what needs to be done

'I have never encountered an executive who remains effective while tackling more than two tasks at a time,' commented the father of modern management, Peter Drucker, who worked with and advised hundreds of managers over his highly productive life.

To show leadership, amongst other things, is to focus on what matters and set priorities. You will continually face choices involving situations and people demanding your attention. (See also Chapter 14.) Correctly choosing where to put your attention and where to stay focused marks you out as a leader, not just someone who implements what other people ask you to do.

Think about what is right for the organisation

Managers who act like leaders think strategically. They see the bigger picture, which can often be decisive in influencing others. By asking, 'What is right for this organisation?' you show you can reach beyond your immediate area of responsibility and avoid the trap of narrow sectional interests.

Thinking strategically is not particularly easy. You probably do not have the full picture and others

thinking strategically is not particularly easy

may even suggest you should not be doing this kind of activity. 'Get back to managing and leave the big issues to us,' is how they might put it, if really pushed. Showing leadership means being willing to step out and being seen to focus on the bigger picture of what is best for the organisation and then acting on it.

Develop action plans

'It's all in my head. I know exactly what should happen and what I want to achieve.' If you are tempted to talk like this, then you risk becoming a prisoner of events. Without a proper action plan in writing, which you can use as a guide and bench mark, you have no real way of knowing which of the events happening around you matter and which do not.

Develop a clear statement of intention, one you are prepared to revise often, talk about constantly and use to make sense of the inevitable and unpredictable opportunities that come your way. The opportunities will doubtless make mincemeat of your intention or, putting it slightly differently, 'To make God laugh talk about your plans.' But creating definite and documented plans in the first place is an important leadership, and certainly management, task.

Take responsibility for decisions

Acting as a leader means holding yourself accountable for essential actions and ones you initiate. Putting it more crudely, you show you are willing to take the blame as well as claiming the credit for success.

Being ready to admit publicly you are wrong, have made the wrong choice, or have made a mistake, can be painful and for some people almost impossible. Yet it is what successful leaders do. They are constantly willing to put themselves on the line, reveal their vulnerability and show they are human and not above messing things up.

Initiate communication

Showing leadership also means you:

◆ make sure action plans are published and fully understood

◆ ask for comments from all colleagues on what needs doing and how

◆ ensure people know what information they need to get the job done

◆ master the information, not letting it master you.

This last requirement is particularly important since the amount of information available is almost infinite. Yet it is seldom more facts that you need: what is vital are knowledge, understanding, interpretation and conclusions.

Focus on opportunities rather than problems

Just about everywhere you look, you will uncover problems. Managers traditionally solve these, spending much of their waking hours coming up with fixes. By contrast, leaders focus more on opportunities and again this can help distinguish you favourably from others around you.

It is not a case of saying, 'Don't bother me with problems, bring me solutions,' which can be an excuse to dump important issues into other people's laps. Instead, you make sure that problems do not overwhelm the opportunities.

Run productive meetings

Every study of what managers actually do confirms that even the newest ones spend more than half their time with other people, that is, in meetings of some kind. Even a conversation with one other person is a meeting.

Effective leaders make their meetings unmissable. They ensure these are work sessions, rather than talking shops or focused exclusively on problems. Show your leadership capability by becoming an expert at running rewarding meetings where people really want to be, rather than merely being required to attend.

Running an effective meeting is not rocket science yet it is surprising how many dreadful meetings happen every day in just about every organisation you can pick on. But it does not have to be like that. (See Chapter 17.)

Think and say 'we' rather than 'I'

You have authority in your organisation because you have gained people's trust. As a leader this means showing clearly that when it comes to your personal needs and opportunities you will put those of the organisation first. This is not at all as easy as it sounds.

It is hard to keep thinking of the organisation rather than your own interests, and many leaders have signally failed to do this. When you say 'we' you show you are putting your ego and your personal desires aside in favour of what is right for your team, your division or the organisation.

Show you care about your people

There are still further practical ways you can demonstrate your leadership, including getting the best from each person, modelling desired behaviour, telling stories, being inspiring and values driven.

Get the best from each person

Be inquisitive about each person who reports to you:

- discover what is unique about them

- know the individual's strengths

- discover the triggers that activate those strengths

- identify the individual's learning style.

great managers spend plenty of time away from their desks

Great managers who show leadership spend plenty of time away from their desks. They walk around, watch people's reactions to events, listen and take mental notes about what attracts each individual's enthusiasm and what they struggle with.

How do you discover these sometimes-elusive facts? Mainly by asking! For example, you might identify a person's strengths by asking: 'What was the best day at work you've had in the past three months? What were you doing and why did you enjoy it so much?' A strength is not just something the person is good at. It is also something they find naturally satisfying and they look forward to doing it repeatedly and getting better at it.

Likewise, ask about the worst day the person experienced in recent months. Probe for details about what they were doing and why they disliked it so much.

Despite the importance of self-awareness, showing leadership does not necessarily mean pushing those you manage to be more self-aware, for example by making them aware of their weaknesses. What counts more than self-awareness is their confidence or self-assurance.

Aim to reinforce confidence, to build self-assurance so the person can persist in the face of obstacles, bounce back when reversals occur and eventually achieve the goals they set. Do this by focusing on the person's strengths and praising their successes not in terms of the hard work involved, but in terms of using their strengths. Put more simply, work to create a state of mind filled with optimism so your people can overcome obstacles and achieve results.

Model desired behaviour

Mahatma Gandhi argued, 'You must be the change you wish to see in the world.' As a leader, people look to you to show them the way, to demonstrate by example how they should behave. Modelling desired behaviour is a challenge, yet is one of the most powerful weapons in your management armoury.

By modelling desired behaviour you provide your people with a visible template against which they create their own actions. Using this template, they gain an understanding of how you will judge them. Contrast this with the more common 'don't do as I do, do as I say' approach, which many managers and leaders adopt and then wonder why they have a hard time making things happen.

The more you advance within an organisation the more important modelling desired behaviours becomes, while proving to be more challenging for you personally. Yet it can be one of the most powerful ways in which to exert your leadership.

Tell stories

Strong leaders tend to be great storytellers. They love bringing their messages to life with personal tales, lively examples, and by talking about their experiences or those of others. In other words, they use stories to capture people's attention and then affect their emotions. When a leader tells a good story it can travel at light speed across the organisation, influencing and affecting people at all levels.

a good story can travel at light speed

While it helps to be a natural raconteur, it is more important that you simply develop your natural ability to bring your key messages to life through stories that entertain and grab people's imagination. Show your leadership by actively searching for and sharing relevant stories with people – stories of success, good practice, exemplary behaviour, outstanding performance, someone making a real difference and so on.

Inspire people

The idea that you might need to inspire people may feel daunting and, for most leaders, it can certainly be a challenge. Yet this lies at the heart of getting the best from people, so you may as well start getting to grips with this issue now. It will become increasingly important as your career develops.

Being inspiring is not necessarily about demonstrating a large charisma, though that can sometimes help. It is more concerned with learning to tap into what moves you, then using it to connect with others, affecting them emotionally and in terms of attitude.

Values driven

Successful leaders repeatedly articulate what they regard as really important, such as shareholder value, integrity, respect for the individual, diversity and so on.

When you are values-driven people soon understand where you are coming from in your communication and in reaching for goals. While these values may partly be based on ones already identified by the organisation, for instance through its mission statement and other such material, it is also important you know and express your own values, and share these with people.

The important point about values is that they help other people make decisions when you are not there – they set the framework within which actions should take place.

Ways to show leadership

☐ *Select what needs to be done*

☐ *Consider what is right for the organisation*

☐ *Develop action plans*

- [ ] *Take responsibility for decisions*
- [ ] *Initiate communication*
- [ ] *Focus on opportunities rather than problems*
- [ ] *Run productive meetings*
- [ ] *Think and say 'we' rather than 'I'*
- [ ] *Be proactive*
- [ ] *Discover what is unique about each person, their strengths and how they best learn*
- [ ] *Reinforce confidence and build self-assurance so people persist in the face of obstacles*
- [ ] *Show by example what you want people to do*
- [ ] *Use stories about success, good practice, exemplary behaviour, outstanding performance and so on*
- [ ] *Learn to tap into what moves you and use this to connect with others*
- [ ] *Be values driven and talk about what matters most to you*
- [ ] *Spend plenty of time away from your desk, walking around connecting with people*

8

Manage your team

WHAT DO THESE COMPANIES HAVE IN COMMON: Johnson & Johnson, L'Oréal, Mars Incorporated, Novartis Oncology, Pfizer and Philip Morris USA? According to recent research, they are all firms with great business teams. In these and other successful teams, power no longer stays locked in one place or in one person. Instead, power sharing is what allows the team to meet its current challenges.

Since managing teams is a core management skill, the essential point is that you need to encourage power sharing; for example, allowing leadership to move around and not rest entirely with you.

If you have ever been a member of a poorly managed team you will almost certainly recall it as a miserable and frustrating experience. Like most managers, therefore, you probably wonder how to get the best from your team. Power is one of the prime ingredients.

power is one of the prime ingredients

Steps to creating a great team

Effective teams consist of more than the sum of their parts. Strong teams seldom just happen and it is one reason for appointing you as a manager – to build an effective team that produces outstanding performance. The good news is that the team itself will almost certainly want you to succeed.

Step 1 – choosing the team members

Your first step towards establishing a well-run team is choosing who should be in it and who should not. You create a successful team rather than inherit it, and only with the right members can you expect to achieve outstanding performance. Traditionally teams use whoever is available. The best teams, those producing a virtuoso performance, choose members for their skills.

Defining team membership can be messy, as you form and reform people into different groupings. Finalising membership may be a sensitive political issue and it helps to clarify:

- the core team members – those whose contribution is necessary over an extended period

- the supporting team members – those who help the team do its work effectively without becoming too involved with the work

- the temporary team members – those whose contribution is usually specific and time-bound.

In the short term, you may indeed inherit your team and feel you have limited scope to alter the membership. It is easy to resent this situation, becoming trigger-happy and taking it out on the team itself or on certain individuals. Instead, set out to assess gradually each team member and their performance and, only if necessary, replace them. Make this a last resort, not the first one.

If you have the freedom to pick your entire team, make the most of it and watch for a natural tendency to choose clones of yourself. Clones are people who seem similar to you in background, thinking and even how they talk. Instead, aim for a healthy diversity, in which you obtain the talent you need in whatever form it comes. (See also Chapter 19.)

Step 2 – developing the team

The second step in managing your team well is recognising that it needs to develop. Sharing your power, that is allowing leadership to move around, will be an important way to encourage the team to move through the essential stages of team development.

Some teams complete the stages shown in the diagram overleaf faster than others, especially with skilled help. Consider using an outside team facilitator; one or two days working together can potentially start transforming the group into a more cohesive and effective unit.

Although the stages of starting, sorting, stabilising, striving, succeeding and stopping may blur into one another, at some point every team needs to go through each one. You cannot always expect the team to remain in the succeeding stage since all teams have ups and down which is why it is so important to keep reviewing how the team views its current performance. Nor can you avoid the stopping stage,

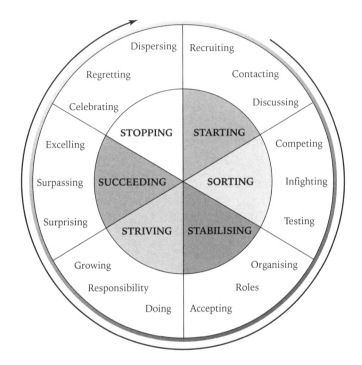

Source: © Maynard Leigh Associates, reproduced with permission.

since every team has a particular life span and at some point needs to recognise it is time to disband and move on.

Step 3 – coaching and encouraging

The third step towards creating a well-run team consists of clarifying your attitude to the individual members. Do you fully respect them, conveying clearly they are special and worth fighting for? With whom are you most happy to share your power? What would make people feel you should manage them?

Acting as the team coach, rather than trying to be a dominant manager or playing the parental role, is yet another way of sharing power and can prove highly productive. As the team coach, you do less managing, concentrate more on supporting, advising, encouraging and listening. This may mean making time for one-to-ones where you help individual members address how they can be more effective within the team.

acting as the team coach is yet another way of sharing power

Step 4 – becoming a team

The fourth essential step moves your people from being merely a group into becoming a team. Groups tend to be weak in areas in which teams become strong. For example, a powerful team will usually:

◆ accept challenging goals

◆ share values

◆ be interdependent

◆ express feelings

◆ rely on commitment rather than control

◆ demonstrate mutual trust

◆ focus on group processes

◆ regularly work in pairs or small groups.

While some groups may show such behaviour, they seldom do it to the same extent as an effective team.

There are practical actions you can take to encourage these team behaviours:

Encourage acceptance of challenging goals: Successful teams thrive on challenging goals. You can be a stimulus to identifying these, encouraging the team to reach beyond its present achievements. If you simply impose these demanding goals, you risk alienating people. Where possible, make setting team goals a joint exercise in which everyone has their say about what to choose. Chapter 14 deals more fully with setting goals.

Sometimes you may find yourself with a non-negotiable aim, perhaps imposed by those more senior in the organisation. Where possible be frank with the team about these imposed goals, sharing the reasoning behind them. Steer your people towards a creative discussion of *how* to reach these goals.

Describing exactly the way you want the team to achieve the goal risks gaining compliance, rather than a wholehearted genuine commitment to strive for the result. (See also Chapter 14.)

Promote shared values: People who feel strongly about the same things tend to bond together, becoming willing to make allowances for each other. This helps the team become more productive.

Make time during team meetings for development sessions that explore personal values, discovering how these relate to those you want to instil in your team. Again, an outside facilitator may be useful in this area.

Encourage interdependence: In strong teams, members come to rely on each other, knowing they can expect support when facing difficult times or significant challenges. Without interdependence, a group seldom transforms into a team.

Support the growth of interdependence with work assignments and communicate how much you value people working together, rather than always competing with each other. Keep referring to successes as due to team effort, rather than constantly praising individuals for achievements towards which everyone has contributed.

Express feelings: Working in a team means people constantly react with each other with plenty of scope for misunderstandings and communication problems. These start to matter if people cannot share their feelings and express concerns or issues openly.

Perhaps, like many managers, you feel uncomfortable dealing with feelings, including your own. Yet an important sign you are succeeding in managing the team is your ability to handle feelings, particularly strong ones. Some powerful ways to do this are:

◆ openly acknowledge the existence of feelings

◆ invite people to talk about them

◆ during normal meetings make room for feelings to be expressed

◆ introduce reality checks – do the facts match up with what people are expressing?

Be willing also to show your own feelings. A heartfelt thank you from the boss is worth as much to some employees as a small pay rise. And many people do not feel sufficiently thanked at work, with a significant number saying they never receive thanks.

Push for commitment rather than control: This arises in numerous ways, particularly through a willingness to play together and to spend social time in each other's company. It can also occur through people making that extra effort, or by supporting each other in their work.

One of the best ways to push for commitment is to model it yourself. Demonstrate your willingness to do whatever it takes to get the job done, while working smarter, not harder. So, for example, take the trouble to find resources for a team member, obtain information that people will find useful, and generally do things for the team that show you are making a special effort on their behalf.

You nearly always face a choice between relying on commitment to get things done and exercising managerial control. Strengthen your team by pushing for commitment to achieving results rather than through being in charge. The latter may temporarily make you feel important but long term it can undermine the power of the team to build a culture of success.

In winning teams, people thrive on autonomy and challenge, rather than constant direction. It is a difficult balance to strike, but worth pursuing. Encourage the emergence of leaders other than yourself. Strangely, the more you achieve shared leadership the stronger you will become as a manager.

> *encourage the emergence of leaders other than yourself*

Demonstrate mutual trust: This is slightly different to just showing commitment. Trust emerges from actions that cumulatively suggest reliability or trustworthiness. A well-run team demonstrates this when members know their colleagues will represent them well in meetings, or stand up for them in difficult situations in public.

Demonstrate trust by showing you can let go while others take responsibility and leadership. For example, do you personally need to chair all team meetings or even always be there? How much oversight do you impose on people? Are you willing to let them decide how best to do things while showing your concern is mainly with results?

Focus on group processes: This is the other side of the coin to being strongly concerned with results. You encourage people to give attention to *how* the group functions. So, for example, guide your team to spend time looking at how to improve meetings, ways the group deals with conflict or relates to other teams.

Looking at the team development diagram again – what stage is your team at? What would move it to the next one, until it is really motoring? What processes seem messy or ineffective, such as setting team goals, how people work together on projects or regular reporting?

Create and work in pairs or small groups: Break large challenges into smaller chunks suitable for tackling by two or three team members working together. Encourage this process by suggesting which pairs or members of the team working together might best produce the desired results. The more you become familiar with the team, the more you will be able to encourage the right mix of skills.

Become a great briefer

A Premier League football team meeting only once a year with its coach would not stay on top for long. Likewise, teams in organisations need to meet regularly, and the briefing process helps people work well together. Everyone gets to share what is happening, solve problems, review progress and set new team challenges.

Experienced managers rate team briefings as one of the best ways to communicate with colleagues and hear their views. The team briefing is an information sharing exercise. You disseminate important news, decisions and issues that could affect how the team manages its future.

Briefing well is a managerial skill, since it is easy to turn such sessions into a lecture or leave people feeling short-changed because there was not enough time to discuss fully the implications. The best briefings are two-way, in which you share information and obtain feedback to help the organisation plan its own long-term future.

Many companies make team briefings part of the culture. They are how the organisation gets things done quickly and are not an optional extra. Companies like Federal Express make such gatherings mandatory and regular. They judge the effectiveness of team managers partly by how good they become at briefing their people.

Briefings need to happen at regular and known intervals, rather than coming unexpectedly only when there is some important announcement. E-mails, video conferences, and webcam conversations can be useful to help with briefing team members but are no substitute for getting the team physically together regularly.

Briefing sessions build your team, strengthen relationships, and promote interdependence and collaborative
working. It pays to hone your briefing skills and the best place
to start is with careful preparation. When you brief your team,
you take centre stage and people want and expect you to
shine. Even talented actors need to rehearse their lines, so
make time to prepare properly. (See also Chapter 4.)

Review progress

Prime ministers, football managers and even pop groups
occasionally need to stand back from the fray and ask the
essential question: 'How are we doing?' If you think your
team is doing fine, then the team review is like a regular
health check. If not, then the team review can be an essential
way to start changing the situation for the better.

The longer the team works together the more sensible it
becomes to explore the basic issue of 'How are we doing?'
Reviews may explore a variety of issues, from 'How do we all
feel right now?' to 'What is stopping us hitting our targets?'
or from 'How do we generate more business?' to 'How well
are our team processes working?' (see box overleaf).

Using a team profile can be an effective way to assess
the team's progress. The well-known Belbin system, for
example, examines what roles people prefer to play in a
team, allowing everyone to explore the implications for team
performance.

Regular team reviews

◆ Identify blocks to joint working

◆ Build relationships; resolve interpersonal difficulties

◆ Give the team fresh momentum

◆ Provide new direction

◆ Keep the team fresh

◆ Inspire people

◆ Improve commitment

◆ Help understand what is happening

◆ Revive a thirst for growth and change

◆ Refocus attention on the big picture

A different approach builds a picture of actual team performance by combining team members' perceptions of how well the group is doing. To describe a successful team, for example, the Maynard Leigh Associates ACE Team Profile relies on 10 essential team processes. Many large organisations use this for obtaining a frank assessment of the team's performance. Each team member fills in an online questionnaire and the combined entries create a visual profile of the team's current performance.

The ACE team profile

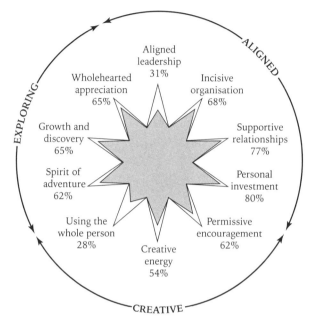

Source: © Maynard Leigh Associates, reproduced with permission.

The team profile and separate ones for each team member highlight where the team is strong and where it may need to concentrate development effort. Encouraging the team to engage in this kind of reflection can help establish you as a thoughtful and challenging team leader. For more about the ACE Team profile, see **www.maynardleigh.co.uk/our-services/on-line-services/**

Ways to manage your team

- [ ] *Check you have the right people in the team*
- [ ] *Make replacing a team member your last resort, not the first one*
- [ ] *Help teams to actively go through the six stages of team development*
- [ ] *See yourself as the team coach, rather than a dominant manager*
- [ ] *Help the team to choose challenging goals*
- [ ] *During team meetings make time to explore personal values*
- [ ] *If necessary, use outside facilitators to promote team growth and change*
- [ ] *Arrange work assignments to generate interdependence*
- [ ] *To promote team openness, be willing to show your own feelings*
- [ ] *Allow leadership to move around the team*
- [ ] *Find ways to demonstrate that you trust the team*
- [ ] *Encourage attention and discussion on how the group functions*
- [ ] *Divide work so a few team members can jointly work on an issue*
- [ ] *Become skilled at delivering regular, interesting team briefings*
- [ ] *Review team progress regularly*

9

Manage your boss

DURING 2008, UK MEMBERS OF PARLIAMENT lambasted BAA's chief executive Colin Mathews over the Terminal 5 fiasco at Heathrow. He publicly admitted he was 'not aware' of problems in the run up to the launch of the multi-billion pound facility. Shortly afterwards, the airport's managing director who reported to Mathews resigned, following a downgrading in a management reshuffle. The manager paid the price, not only for the debacle, but also for not keeping his boss fully informed.

Four critical mistakes new or inexperienced managers make are:

1 Being excessively compliant – 'I just need to do what the boss wants'.

2 Demonising – 'I don't trust her/him'.

3 Being target obsessed – 'I'm bound to succeed if I consistently hit my targets'.

4 Being relationship blind – 'All that matters is getting the job done'.

These are negative behaviours. Equally there are some positive behaviours that will help you manage upwards.

Under-promise and over-deliver

While getting the job done may not be the sole concern of your boss (see above), it will still play a vital part in how well you work together. Make it a personal rule to under-promise and over-deliver.

you may find yourself facing a non-negotiable goal

The results you commit to delivering will normally stem from one or more discussions. Occasionally, though, you may find yourself facing a non-negotiable goal, chosen and imposed by someone else. Externally set goals, such as sales targets, can be uncomfortable, even oppressive. But, unless you are willing to resign, somehow you will probably end up attempting to reach them.

What counts is making a genuine attempt to succeed, going that extra mile, doing everything possible to deliver – and being seen to do that. (See also Chapter 14.)

Manage expectations

Passively assuming you know instinctively what the boss wants could create problems. Explore actively the other person's expectations, if necessary asking them to spell out clearly what they want.

Some superiors can explain their expectations in detail, others cannot. If necessary, seek a meeting where you jointly examine the whole issue of expectations. You may even have to lead the way with direct questions such as:

- 'What results are you expecting from me this next quarter?'

- 'What would make you feel I was being really effective in this job?'

- 'What kind of problems do you want to be informed about and when?'

- 'What information do you need before the project is completed?'

Getting a person who tends to be vague to express their expectations can be hard work. One solution is to draft a detailed note covering the key aspects and send it for their approval. Follow this up with a request for a face-to-face discussion in which you go over each item. This kind of discussion will often bring to the surface the other person's expectations, such as:

- 'I want you to deliver agreed results on time and show a degree of leadership while doing so.'

- 'I need to be kept fully informed about what you are doing.'

- 'I expect to be told of any new issues or situations you encounter that might affect my own role or effectiveness.'

- 'I rely on you to be my ears and eyes across the division.'

- 'You're great at dealing with people, I depend on you to give me early warning if someone or the team feels unhappy about the way things are going.'

Whatever the expectations, it is your job to unravel them, becoming as clear as you can about them. For example, you may need to become assertive and challenge the boss about the urgency of a request with, 'Let me show you my current to-do list so we can agree what to remove from it to allow me to deliver on this timescale.'

Just as the boss will have expectations, you will have some of your own and what you want from the relationship. For example, you may consider it essential to have a regular weekly or monthly meeting to review progress and share useful information. Or you may need extra support when trying to deliver a particularly difficult result. Share these expectations. Do not assume the other person somehow already knows them.

Anticipate

Successful managers thrive by being ahead of the game, anticipating demands and guessing correctly what their bosses want next from them. You do not need to be a mind reader to do this.

◆ Become familiar with how the other person thinks and behaves.

◆ Stay alert to what is happening around you.

◆ Discover issues and problems your boss is currently experiencing.

◆ Keep the boss informed.

Look for evidence of what the boss seems most concerned about and then seek opportunities to discuss this.

For example, if you realise your boss is anxious about some issue, what contribution could you make to help reduce this concern? Simply being a good listener may be all that you need do in some cases. If you realise that before attending a regular senior meeting your boss tends to fuss excessively, demanding lots of information, you could enquire well in advance whether there is anything you can do to help.

Finally, keep the boss fully informed and avoid surprises.

Invest in the relationship

Otherwise talented managers sometimes ignore the crucial importance of nurturing their relationship with their own bosses. If you have previously had a good, understanding boss, it may be a shock to find yourself with one who is not. The critical importance of the upward relationship is not always obvious, until some misunderstanding or confusion arises. For instance, a miscommunication may cause a planning activity to go wrong and if the relationship is weak, mutual recriminations can follow.

If you do not get on with your boss, it can be tempting to dismiss it as merely a clash of personalities. But this could mean you avoid facing up to factors that are more within your control. The real cause may not be your different personalities, but unrealistic assumptions and expectations about the nature of the relationship. To survive and thrive as a manager it is important to recognise you are mutually dependent on each other and are both fallible human beings.

you are mutually dependent on each other

With a clear understanding of both your boss and yourself, you can usually establish a way of working together that fits both of you. This means recognising different work styles. For example, it makes sense to adjust your approach to the other person's preferred method of receiving information. Some bosses like to receive information in report form, so they can read and study it. Others work better through information delivered in person, so they can ask questions.

If your boss is a listener give a full briefing followed by a written report, e-mail or memo. If your boss is a reader, cover important items or proposals in written form, *and then* discuss them.

Creating a compatible relationship also involves drawing on each other's strengths and making up for each other's weaknesses. For example, if you know your boss is rather weak on follow-through, offer to do this yourself or provide monitoring reports. Enquiring about the pressures your boss is under is not being unduly nosey. It shows you want to be supportive and understanding when adverse behaviour strikes.

Some basic errors inexperienced managers make when trying to manage upwards are taking information supplied by the boss at face value, making assumptions in areas where they have no information and not clarifying the boss's objective.

Finally, go above your boss at your peril! (See also below.) The organisation has a big stake in this person's success so going over their head must be an absolutely last resort and certainly not just to get your way or win points.

Take the initiative

From your boss's perspective, knowing you do not always wait passively to receive orders can be reassuring. It builds trust and mutual reliance. If you feel you need permission before you can do anything out of the ordinary, it suggests the relationship needs some serious attention.

If something goes wrong, offer your own solutions first – do not wait to be found out. Admittedly, this carries risks as some bosses hate hearing bad news and only want to know when things are going well. This merely means you need to find ingenious ways to get the information across in an acceptable form.

There is a considerable difference, though, between taking the initiative and becoming a loose cannon where your actions are unpredictable and cause unnecessary problems. When using your initiative take time to inform the boss about you actions, inviting comments or discussion about your intentions.

Few things are more disabling for a boss than having a subordinate who is undependable, whose work cannot be trusted. When you take the initiative, it needs to be within the context of delivering the agreed goals, rather than going off on some new direction of your own choosing.

Dealing with an out-of-control boss

Almost everyone has times when the boss seems to have gone crazy. Usually it is a one-off or temporary situation, due to office politics or a personal crisis. But sometimes the resulting behaviour may threaten your team, department or even the company. So what do you do when the boss becomes a problem person?

The reason for being out of control hardly matters. In this uncomfortable situation, the most sensible goal is damage limitation, with clients, employees, suppliers and others. Most of all you want to ensure your work and results continue.

You are almost certainly not alone in seeing the issue. Others also experiencing the problem boss could be subordinates, peers or those higher up the line. Action you can take includes the following.

Prioritise and get on with the work

Do not get distracted with all the ramifications of this problem person. Instead, focus on rallying your team, keeping the boss informed about work problems. Meanwhile take cautious soundings to check whether key influencers like HR people and other functional heads are aware of what is going on.

Raise the issue intelligently

When the boss is reasonable and functioning normally, it is easy to put forward your position and raise problems. It takes courage to do this when the boss has become a problem person and off balance. Colleagues and team members could see doing nothing as weakness.

Control the grape vine

Until the boss recovers, leaves or otherwise changes for the better, remain supportive. Do not give others details, they will know soon enough about the problems. Much the same goes for suppliers and customers: be circumspect about what you say and how you say it.

Know your limit

A problem boss can make life hell and you need to set a deadline on how long you will continue working with this person. Weak managers let this issue drift and consequently may end up suffering for months, even years. What matters is being proactive, which might include organising a move to a boss elsewhere in the same organisation, joining a project team where your boss has less direct power over you or even making plans to leave.

a problem boss can make life hell

Sit it out

You may decide that because your boss will soon leave or retire, the best strategy is to sit it out and wait. Depending on the timescale, this will be viable only if it does not adversely affect how peers and senior colleagues will judge you.

Initiate contact further up the line

Like resignation, this is almost certainly a last resort strategy and high risk. Do it only when everything else has failed. Top management has a substantial stake in your boss so consider extremely carefully the political ramifications of bypassing your immediate manager.

If you decide to go up the line, present your case in terms of impact on the bottom line; stick to the facts and make no sweeping accusations; do not ask that 'something be done'. (See also Chapter 13.)

Ways to manage your boss

☐ *Discover how your boss sees their current goals and pressures*

☐ *Make sure you know the person's strengths and weaknesses*

☐ *Develop actively and maintain the relationship*

☐ *Clarify mutual expectations*

☐ *Keep your boss informed*

☐ *Avoid seeking help with trivial issues, use your boss's time sparingly*

☐ *Become a coach to your manager*

☐ *Value your boss's political capital and use it sparingly*

☐ *Under-promise and over-deliver*

☐ *If you cannot meet a deadline say so sooner rather than later*

☐ *Even if you can do your boss's job, do not go around boasting about it*

☐ *Respond to questions and treat them with respect*

☐ *Do not broadcast your boss's failings*

☐ *Defuse criticism or personal attacks with your sense of humour*

☐ *Offer solutions not problems*

☐ *Show you're a chooser rather than a blamer*

☐ *Offer ways to get the best out of yourself; don't have it dragged out of you*

☐ *Recognise the relationship reflects mutual dependency and honesty*

10

Review performance

'I NEVER READ MY REVIEWS,' claimed Woody Allen at the 2002 Cannes Film Festival. 'I never see my movies. I never look at anything about myself. I keep myself ostrich-like.'

Famous film directors may be able to ignore their reviews and behave like an ostrich, but in the corporate world, for most people the universal answer to the basic question, 'How am I doing?' seems to be 'We would rather not tell you!'

At the prospect of conducting a performance review, many managers allow their imagination to run riot. They think those they manage will respond to even the mildest comment with stone walling, anger or tears. Subordinates too fear they will hear only criticism. The result? Everyone keeps quiet, saying as little as possible. The formal annual appraisal therefore has few friends. Critics label it 'one of the seven deadly sins of management' and one calls it 'a modern-day bloodletting'.

subordinates fear they will hear only criticism

Yet it is vital to show people how they are doing in their work. Prior to a cultural overhaul at the retailer John Lewis, for example, managers were overprotective and tolerant of poor performance. As one senior executive explains, 'It was neither kind nor honest, since it was not giving employees the chance to improve their performance and pay, or generate the careers they wanted.'

To make your performance reviews work, keep them regular, get clear about their purpose and steer those you manage to establish their own performance goals using a variety of techniques.

Make it regular

A solitary annual appraisal makes little sense. If this is how your organisation operates, underpin it with your own, far more frequent sessions reviewing performance and giving feedback. Frequent performance reviews allow you to turn them into enjoyable developmental sessions. In genuine developmental sessions, you ignore issues like salary setting or complaints about minor performance issues. Instead, you concentrate on the person's total development. This can be a mutually satisfying and creative experience. It allows you fully to explore how to help the other person perform to their full potential.

In a well-run development session, for instance, you focus on broad issues, like where is the person heading in their career, what help do they need to develop, such as training or further work experience, what might be getting in the way of improving performance and so on.

Make it clear

Irregularity turns the occasional formal review session into a daunting event. There is too much at stake with little clarity about what the session will try to achieve.

Purpose of performance review systems: Perceived importance vs actual experience

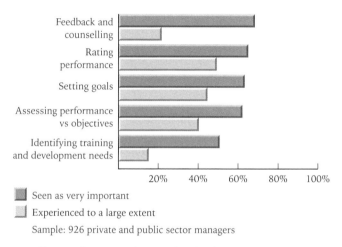

Seen as very important

Experienced to a large extent

Sample: 926 private and public sector managers

Source: Strebler, M., Robinson, D. and Bevan, S. (2001) *Performance Review: Balancing Objectives and Content*, Institute for Employment Studies, Report 370, February. Reproduced with permission.

Clarify the purpose of the session for the other person. For example, in one of the world's largest consultancies, there is at least one session every year when managers must rank each individual they are responsible for on a corporate ladder. Everyone either has someone above them, or below them, and the session focuses almost entirely on arriving at this decision.

Make it well-prepared

Faced with performance reviews, those on the receiving end often say they would rather visit the dentist or fill in a tax return. People will look forward to the session with you only if they realise you will be:

◆ well prepared, having given thought to what you want to say, or how best to say it

◆ clear about the objectives and without a mixed agenda

◆ willing to be frank about how you view the person's performance.

Invest quality time in preparing for reviews. Gather and structure the evidence into an orderly presentation that will make sense to the person you meet.

Make it forward looking

Look Back in Anger was the title of a famous play, but with performance reviews the less you look back the better. Instead, treat the process as cyclical with little time spent looking backwards. Certainly celebrate successes with praise, but keep your focus on helping people achieve their next goals, offering continuous feedback, coaching and training.

concentrate on the future

The more you look back, the more people may regard it as either unfair, ill-informed or irrelevant. The more you concentrate on the future, the greater the chance the meeting will be productive.

Start with aspirations

Many appraisals fail because they use a reward and punishment approach. Instead, start with the individual's own aspirations, and how they see themselves developing. Find ways to relate these to what the organisation wants to achieve.

Different people respond to different approaches to performance improvement so be prepared to adapt to what they find most useful.

◆ Tell and sell – *'Here's what I think about your work and I'd like you to try my suggestions for action.'* This approach is highly directive and works best with those having the least work experience.

◆ Tell and listen – *'I'll explain how I see your work and after that it's up to you to say what you think.'* This approach at least shares your views of performance, but makes the session one-sided and will not necessarily enrol the other person in taking action.

◆ Joint problem solving – *'We'll discuss work problems and possible solutions; together we'll work out what to do.'* As long as it is a genuine discussion then this approach can work well, engaging the other person in a shared approach to suitable action.

◆ Self-appraisal – *'You tell me how effective you think you are since you'll be much tougher on yourself than I'll ever be. I'll add my thoughts to yours for further action.'* This approach puts the onus on the other person to say how they see their performance. It works well so long as you are frank about how you view their performance and do not leave it entirely up to them to arrive at a conclusion.

◆ Goal setting – *'We'll set some mutually acceptable goals and decide how we'll monitor progress. If you want I'll suggest ways of achieving these goals.'* With the growth of knowledge workers and the decline of hierarchy the big shift is towards this approach where people establish their own performance goals. Managers are simply there to ensure these goals have an organisational context.

(See also Chapter 14.)

Make it honest

Most of us would rather duck the issue of telling someone they have done something badly, focusing instead on the good points. Yet it is this tendency which explains why people often view appraisals with such contempt.

According to research by YouGov, on behalf of Investors in People, a third of employees in the UK consider appraisals a complete waste of time and nearly half think their bosses evade home truths when conducting an annual assessment. Almost one in four says the process is unfair.

To be useful, your appraisal meetings must not become disguised disciplinary hearings. Nor are they a chance to get your own back or be a salary-setting exercise without acknowledging it. The more you clarify the exact purpose of the review process the greater the chance of it affecting the person's actual work performance.

Make it purposeful

Appraisals are universally unpopular partly because they try to do too many things at once. While your own review efforts may rightly focus on immediate work performance, it is also important to consider the big picture: Does this person support our company culture, its values and aspirations? Instead of asking, 'Are you doing what I asked?' ask 'What are you doing to support our vision and our values?'

Even if you are stuck with a lumbering formal appraisal system this does not stop you starting with an important assumption that people come to work to succeed, not to fail.

Try to widen your approach to reviews so they generate powerful and useful conversations. Rather than passing judgement, focus on:

- offering direction
- recognising and rewarding
- discovering employee concerns
- offering and receiving feedback
- increasing job satisfaction
- sharing knowledge.

This is likely to be more satisfying than ticking boxes or scoring the person using some dubious rating system. In this form of appraisal you take on the more useful roles of leader, facilitator, negotiator, counsellor and even researcher.

Make it two-way

One of the best ways to transform the performance review is by making it a genuinely two-way experience. This is admittedly more demanding than simply telling someone about their performance, since you become open to hearing uncomfortable feedback about your own performance as a talent manager – 'How am I doing at getting the best from you?'

make it a genuinely two-way experience

By making it a two-way review, with a genuine desire to learn how you might help the person improve, you gain invaluable information about how you can develop as a manager and leader. For example, you may fondly believe that you are accessible and easy to reach. In the two-way exchange, you may discover people find you less available than you think. Or you may believe you give clear instructions for work tasks, only to learn in the exchange that you could be much clearer.

Using a two-way review process, you have the opportunity to encourage the other person to prepare for the encounter. Explain that you want to know where they find you strong or weak in helping them perform their job well. This also moves the review away from blaming company problems on individuals, to focusing on the quality of the management they receive. Also, if you only deal with the individual's issues without a wider company context you may simply damage morale.

Make it real

Effective reviews work best when based on hard evidence. People need concrete examples of behaviour, attitude or choices that make your case about performance. This is why preparation is so important since it gives you time to gather these live examples from actual experience.

Vague assertions such as 'you could try harder' or 'you have the wrong attitude' leave you open to accusations of bias, being uninformed about the person's actual performance or relying on hearsay. Obtain solid facts and examples from peer assessments, discussions with colleagues, rating scales and tests of competencies, and evaluate individual results against agreed goals.

Make it logical

One of the secrets of doing a review well is creating a definite structure so that both parties know the territory you will be covering (see also above). A typical structure you might adopt would be as follows.

◆ Introduction – *'How are we going to go about this together?'*

◆ Discuss performance strength – *'Which areas have you done really well in recently?'*

◆ Review areas for personal development – *'What areas of performance should you improve or develop?'*

◆ Create specific plans – *'What action do we need to set in motion and by when?'*

◆ Summarise – *'These are the key points we have discussed and agreed.'*

There are plenty of other ways to do it. What matters is giving the encounter a logical progression, moving from one issue to the next in a planned way. This provides reassurance that you will not skate over or miss out anything important.

Start the whole review process with a written agenda and to complete it allow at least 60–90 minutes. Follow it up with a written report detailing the decisions and give the other person an opportunity to comment on it.

Use the power of self-assessment

As we have seen, people may require help to obtain the feedback they need. Self-assessment can be a powerful way to encourage them to take responsibility for the review process, for instance asking colleagues for feedback.

Self-assessment can be tough, particularly if the person has never previously received useful feedback. First, invite them to decide for themselves which elements of their job are the most important. Secondly, ask them to recall any informal feedback they have received from colleagues, subordinates and customers – not only words, but facial expressions, body language, and silences. For example, can they recall both negative and positive examples of how people reacted to them in recent meetings, or whether people seem pleased to interact with them, either one-to-one or in groups?

A self-generated review helps the person begin to recognise there has already been positive informal feedback from many of those with whom they interact.

Some people may be shy or reluctant to speak about strengths and overplay their weaknesses. Encourage a balanced discussion about strengths and reframe weaknesses in a

encourage a balanced discussion

positive way: 'It's true you say little in meetings, but you always seem to give everyone your full attention.'

Use active listening (see Chapter 2) to detect repeated statements or key words, indicating you may not have correctly heard an issue, understood it or perhaps not seen its importance. Summarise and rephrase the point and ask if you have understood it correctly.

Finally, compare the person's own perception of their performance with your own view of it. This is when you offer your balanced picture of their strengths and developmental needs. Self-assessment provides a useful context for this type of feedback.

Ways to review performance

☐ *Conduct performance reviews regularly, rather than annually*

☐ *Prepare carefully for each review*

☐ *Set a time for giving the person your undivided attention with no interruptions*

☐ *Communicate clearly the purpose of the appraisal process*

☐ *Start with the person's aspirations and how they see themselves developing*

☐ *Be frank about performance, offering honest feedback that people can use*

☐ *Talk about successes not only failures, strengths not just weaknesses*

☐ *Make the location for the review pleasant and relaxing*

☐ *Assess 'What are you doing to support our vision and our values?'*

☐ *Do not play judge and jury; take more useful roles of leader, facilitator, negotiator, counsellor and even researcher*

☐ *Make it into a two-way experience*

☐ *Ask, 'How can I make your job easier for you?' and 'How might I manage you better?'*

☐ *Focus on the future rather than dwelling on the past*

☐ *Rely on evidence, rather than judgement or assertions*

☐ *Create a clear structure so you both know the review territory*

☐ *Use the power of self-assessment*

11

Coach for results

THE JOKES JUST KEEP COMING. Everyone in your team laughs, but in a rather strained way since the humour usually comes at someone's expense. You could tell the team comedian to stop it, hoping a gentle slap-on-the-wrist will work. But what if the jokes continue? The joker in your team would be a prime candidate for one-to-one coaching, helping them to use their abundant humour more appropriately. As a way of improving people's performance, coaching is now widely accepted as a core skill for virtually all managers.

coaching is now widely accepted as a core skill

You may need to coach at any time, offering coaching to virtually anyone who values your support, including your boss. It also differs in important ways from everyday management. While managers provide direction and make the best use of resources, as a coach you focus on showing people how they can do it themselves. It is the equivalent of teaching someone to fish, rather than merely handing over dead fish.

The best management coaches focus on achieving specific results usually based around improving work performance. Coaching involves a less hierarchical relationship than the managerial one, and it's less directive. It is more like a carefully arranged conversation, based on mutual respect with a shared wish to grow and develop. The quality of the conversation determines whether you make any difference to the person's actual behaviour.

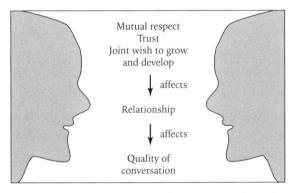

Source: *Be a High Performance Coach: A Solutions Guide.* © Maynard Leigh Associates, 2005, reproduced with permission.

Unlike managing change in the broader organisational sense (see Chapter 15) the power of coaching lies in helping to change an individual's behaviour to improve their effectiveness. Quite simply, when you coach well you help people understand how to succeed.

The mentor versus coach relationship is shown in the table opposite.

Mentor	Coach
On-going and long-term	Short-term focus
Recipient describes need	Coach may suggest needs
Teacher	Trainer
Not directly accountable	Directly accountable if a line manager
Works on personal and professional issues	Concentrates on job-related issues

I don't want to coach!

While every manager needs to learn to coach for results, not everyone takes to the idea of coaching. Many find it time-consuming and regard the process as mysterious, with uncertain outcomes. Reluctance to coach often stems from a fear of being candid, and inadequate personal boundaries.

Candour

To be a good coach you need to be frank with the other person about their performance. Candour, though, can generate emotion, which for some managers feels intensely scary. The best antidote to this fear starts with respecting the other person. Do they actually want you to be candid? When would be the most appropriate time to give them feedback on which to base the coaching conversation? In what form would they find factual feedback most useful – for example, as questions, as straight information, as stories?

Personal boundaries

Fear of overstepping personal boundaries also explains resistance to being a coach. For example, it may feel like assuming too much responsibility for someone's performance. 'I'm a manager, not a therapist' is how some people justify avoiding the coaching role. Yet good coaching is about discovery, not therapy. It uses many of the skills of basic management, including emotional intelligence (EI), listening, questioning, persuasion, goal setting and managing meetings.

As a coach, by focusing on results you strengthen the boundaries around the conversation held with the other person. You do not try to change their personality, only how they go about producing results at work.

Outside help

You could consider outsourcing the job to a specialist. But not being able to coach for results may eventually damage your career. As you progress, you will be increasingly working with people who you cannot command what to do. To obtain the best from them will mean adopting a coaching style. (See also Chapter 13.)

The five stages

You may find it useful to attend a development workshop. This will allow you to practise coaching safely and discover its power. Think of it as a five-stage process: prepare, assess, explore, practise and review.

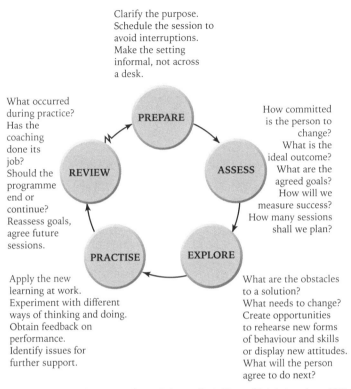

Clarify the purpose. Schedule the session to avoid interruptions. Make the setting informal, not across a desk.

PREPARE

How committed is the person to change? What is the ideal outcome? What are the agreed goals? How will we measure success? How many sessions shall we plan?

ASSESS

What are the obstacles to a solution? What needs to change? Create opportunities to rehearse new forms of behaviour and skills or display new attitudes. What will the person agree to do next?

EXPLORE

Apply the new learning at work. Experiment with different ways of thinking and doing. Obtain feedback on performance. Identify issues for further support.

PRACTISE

What occurred during practice? Has the coaching done its job? Should the programme end or continue? Reassess goals, agree future sessions.

REVIEW

Source: *Be a High Performance Coach: A Solutions Guide.* © Maynard Leigh Associates, 2005, reproduced with permission.

These various stages need not be complicated or lengthy. But they can make the coaching process more systematic, predictable and for the person on the receiving end more reassuring. The five-stage process is particularly useful when you conduct formal coaching activity, perhaps over several months.

It is worth explaining to the other person the various stages of how coaching works. This allows them to adjust their expectations, giving them confidence in you – you know the journey on which you are taking them.

Action-focused coaching (AFC)

A short, informal, coaching session may not need the full five-stage approach: for instance, when you encounter someone by a coffee machine, chat briefly after a meeting or conduct a telephone conversation. Informal though these encounters may be, you still may be coaching in various ways.

Action-focused coaching (AFC) focuses on an easy to recall structure of objectives, obstacles and action (see figure below).

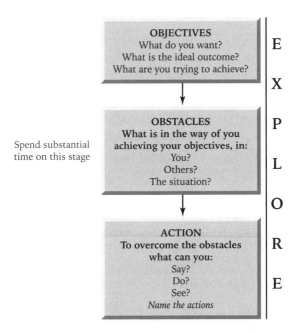

Source: *Be a High Performance Coach: A Solutions Guide.* © Maynard Leigh Associates, 2005, reproduced with permission.

This structure is easy to recall and allows you to work through the issue systematically.

During the final action stage, you do not dictate the action. Instead, you encourage the person to discover for themselves the various possibilities, selecting the best course as they see it, not necessarily as you see it.

Listening

'Show me a coach, or a boss, who doesn't listen – really listen – and I'll show you a probable loser,' commented Brad Gilbert, the outstanding professional tennis player who became the top tennis coach of World Champions Andre Agassi and Andy Roddick. (See also Chapter 2.)

When coaching for results you pay close attention, showing you are alert by words and body language. You do not simply sit back and merely act like a sponge. If you are a specialist or expert in some area, you may be used to listening and then producing answers for people. Coaching does not work that way, since you avoid telling people what to do, instead helping them to discover the answers for themselves.

So, when acting as a coach avoid acting the know-it-all or responding with, 'Here's what I think you should do.' Instead, listen intently, then steer people towards finding the solution for themselves. Short term, this hands-off approach requires more time than giving them immediate answers. However, longer-term, effective coaching encourages people to be self-reliant and therefore make fewer demands on you.

Limit your critical tendencies

Without looking, try chucking a tennis ball over your head behind you, making it drop into an empty waste bin a few feet away. Now imagine someone reporting on your efforts like this: 'That was absolutely terrible; you completely missed the bin, miles out!' Now, imagine doing it again, but this time the other person reports: 'You were six inches too far to the left and about a foot too long.' Which do you think is more helpful to someone who wants to improve their performance at getting the ball in the bin?

curb any tendency to judge people

In management coaching, you may need to curb any tendency to judge people and instead give them an accuracy check. For example, is the person describing reality about their performance, are the facts correct, are they interpreting the situation positively or negatively?

Good management coaches ruthlessly separate facts from interpretation. Reflect back on what you think you have heard, and only then offer an interpretation.

Feedback

Feedback lies at the heart of coaching and leaves people feeling supported. To give useful feedback:

- ◆ acknowledge the person's feelings or viewpoint

- ◆ focus on potential improvements not mistakes

- ◆ stick to observable facts

- ◆ concentrate on required behaviours, not personality.

Great management coaches learn how to offer feedback in ways that the other person can accept. Sometimes this comes as engaging stories that inspire the other person to think differently about an issue, or it may happen through well-directed questions (see the section below). Alternatively, it may come in the form of helping the other person interpret evidence already in their possession: for example, 'You say people seldom really contribute much during your meetings. What do you think this is telling us about what is happening?'

Effective feedback works best when the other person feels ready to receive it. You need to work at preparing them to receive the information you wish to impart. For example, suppose you feel someone gives terrible presentations. While you could simply tell them your opinion, it may be far more effective to insist the person first conducts some personal enquiries into the effectiveness of their presentations. Having discovered there is considerable room for improvement, the person may then be more ready to receive your coaching on ways to improve their performance.

Questions

Helping someone discover ways to improve their performance will often depend on the questions you ask. Pose them in a spirit of curiosity and exploration, not as if conducting an inquisition into their behaviour.

Powerful coaching questions will have the following qualities.

- **Non-judgemental** – you do not infer a right or wrong answer, instead you leave the other with options to explore.
  'How might you improve your presentation next time?'

- **Simple and succinct** – you avoid complex questions suggesting you are an expert, instead you keep the questions short and simple allowing the other person to start tackling them.
  'What do think is the main point of the presentation?'

- **Open** – these do not elicit a simple yes or no response since this kind of response will often stifle the coaching conversation abruptly.
  'How can I help you?' or *'Tell me about your current role?'*

- **In tune with the other's thinking** – you choose a style of communication with which the other person can most easily connect.
  'Do you feel good about that?'
  'What do you think of that?'
  'Is that what you hear from your colleagues?'

- **Reflective** – check your understanding and the underlying feelings.
  'You seem to be angry about it, is that right?'

Challenge

Entire companies often respond well to what researcher and writer Jim Collins called Big Hairy and Audacious Goals. Equally, individuals may best improve their work performance through a coaching challenge. 'Treat people as if they are what they ought to be, and you help them become what they are capable of being,' argued the poet Goethe.

Before offering a coaching challenge, check first with your own internal coach. Are you doing it from a genuine desire to help the other person, or a wish to punish them in some way? If you feel a strong urge to tell the other person a few home truths, something you have wanted to do for a long time, then you are not in a coaching mode at all.

There are various ways to challenge without sounding as if you are out to 'get' the other person in some way. These include the following.

◆ **Confrontation** – rather than ignore difficult behaviour, instead you name it, explaining to the person what they are doing and why it is unacceptable.
'You keep interrupting people in meetings and it is making our meetings less enjoyable.'

◆ **Specific questions** – these challenge the person directly.
'Do you know why you get so angry when someone suggests you are wrong?'

◆ **State expectations** – say, clearly, what you want to happen.
'As we need you to work strictly within your budget next month, let's discuss how you can achieve that.'

◆ **Create boundaries** – people want to know what is acceptable at work, and your coaching session may need to set out the limits.
'It is hard to be constantly positive, but constant moaning in team meetings is not acceptable around here.'

In adopting a supporting, enabling style during coaching, there is always a danger of moving too far in this direction and losing sight of your essential managerial role. When the situation demands it, such as a mission-critical task, where failure would lead to disaster, you may need to demonstrate tough management. Here you show what you want and communicate clearly what you expect to change. (See also Chapter 13.)

Resistance

People will resist your coaching if they feel it will be punishing, concerned mainly with their faults, or an entirely one-sided conversation. Resistance also arises when someone feels, 'There's nothing wrong with me?' or asks, 'Why do I need any coaching?' This can be a delicate situation to resolve. An effective solution can be to separate initial problem description feedback strictly from any subsequent coaching sessions.

First, show convincingly why the person needs to change in some way, presenting them with clear factual evidence. For example:

◆ 'In your last three presentations the audience were unclear what your main point was. It seems you could benefit from some help on this issue.'

◆ 'This is the fourth time you have promised to deliver something on time but not met your commitment. We need to tackle this issue before it damages your career.'

Secondly, offer formal coaching only when the person agrees there is an issue to resolve.

Learning to coach

There are many workshops where you can safely practise coaching. During them, you will discover how to give feedback sensitively, influence with integrity, learn to trust your intuition and build the relationship.

Ways to coach for results

☐ *Make it a two-way affair in which you also develop*

☐ *Avoid telling people what to do, help them discover the answer*

☐ *Use the five-stage process: prepare, assess, explore, practise and review*

☐ *For quick coaching use objectives, obstacles and action*

☐ *Explore and learn to use known effective coaching techniques*

☐ *Listen actively*

☐ *Employ your intuition*

☐ *Ask questions in a positive way*

☐ *Influence with integrity*

☐ *Give feedback sensitively*

☐ *Show empathy despite setbacks*

☐ *Show compassion*

☐ *Work collaboratively*

☐ *Focus on action*

12

Negotiate successfully

IF YOU COULD QUIZ SHERLOCK HOLMES for the secret of his success, he would probably murmur, 'It's elementary.' The more obliging, equally fictitious detective Hercule Poirot might twiddle his gleaming black moustache and explain he spots and interprets clues that lesser mortals miss. Becoming a successful negotiator is like being a Sherlock Holmes or Hercule Poirot. You constantly search for clues to give your negotiations an edge. For behind the endless, deal-driven headlines, managers constantly negotiate. They bargain with customers and suppliers, with large shareholders, with potential alliance partners and with people inside their companies.

As Bob Davis, once CEO of the Spanish communications company Lycos put it: 'Companies have to make deal making a core competency.' You probably already know the basics of negotiating and may even be particularly good at it. Yet according to professor and negotiation expert James Sebenius, high stakes and intense pressure can cause costly mistakes. 'I'm struck by how frequently even experienced negotiators leave money on the table, deadlock, damage relationships or allow conflict to spiral.'

As a negotiation detective, be nosy. To understand the other side's problem, keep asking probing questions, and listen intently. And, like the TV sleuth Columbo, regardless of your outward manner, do it all from an inner confidence.

keep asking probing questions

Confidence at bargaining stems first from doing plenty of it. Secondly, it comes from knowing and using the learnable habits of effective negotiation, described below. Since most organisations regard highly those who can successfully negotiate, using these habits is an important way to thrive as a manager.

When it happens

Like a crime detective, you will encounter various types of cases. These include the following.

Informal occasions

> **'I want this report by Tuesday, how can we make that happen?'**
>
> **'If I chair the meeting, will you handle the time-keeping?'**

Informal bargaining occurs so often one hardly thinks twice about it. For instance, it is the start of informal negotiations if you ask your team to complete a job by midweek and they argue for doing it by the end of the week, or if you tell the boss you need a pay rise and only receive a non-committal response.

Formal negotiations

These may stem from informal ones. They involve bosses, trade unions and other bodies and can be over wages, working arrangements or some area of activity.

> *'If we provide you with the full data, would you hold off action until next month?'*
>
> *'We need more flexibility in overtime working; will your members accept that in exchange for a guarantee of a minimum amount monthly?'*

Negotiations with a trade union or other representative bodies will seldom be informal, except perhaps early on. Usually these encounters become like a carefully choreographed dance, with everyone knowing the right moves.

Commercial bargaining

This aims to achieve a business deal, for example a new contract with a supplier, a merger arrangement, tackling the terms of a sale.

> *'At what price would you consider committing to a five-year contract with us?'*
>
> *'Our cancellation arrangements differ from your proposed procurement contract; can we explore how to resolve this?'*

Negotiations fail for as many reasons as there are individuals and deals. Yet there are several common mistakes which, with care, you can certainly avoid.

Classic negotiation mistakes

◆ **Don't bother understanding the other side's problem.** You can only negotiate effectively if you understand both your own interests and those of your counterpart. You need to address these as a way of solving your own problem.

◆ **Make price dominate everything.** If you focus exclusively on price you turn potentially cooperative deals into adversarial ones. This is a common mistake of inexperienced managers fixated on creating win/lose outcomes.

◆ **Neglect the best alternative.** You may be better off with no deal at all. It may be better to walk away, prolong a stalemate, make something in-house instead, procure a product externally, or write it off.

◆ **Skewed vision.** You may feel you see the negotiation situation clearly, yet like a pilot's sense of the horizon at night, it can be wildly wrong. Misreading the situation leads to negotiation errors.

Most negotiations are like a six-act stage play. The curtain goes up after lots of rehearsals – that is, intense preparations. Then the first actors appear, setting the scene and, in negotiation terms, making the initial offer. The real show begins when the actors strut their stuff, which in negotiation terms is about clarifying the situation so everyone knows what is going on. As each scene unfolds, we usually see lots of interaction – the bargaining stage. The curtain comes down with some kind of resolution – the close of the negotiation. Once the performance ends, the cast continues making improvements, which in negotiation terms is follow-through or implementation.

These six scenes – prepare, offer, clarify, bargain, close and implement – may blur at the edges, occurring quickly without gaps between them. But make sure you keep track of where you are in the entire negotiation.

Invest in preparation

Golfing legend Gary Player once explained: 'The more I prac-tise, the luckier I get.' Several millennia earlier Sun Tzu, writing about the art of warfare, put it slightly differently: 'Every battle is won before it is ever fought.'

Research into negotiation usually focuses on the cut and thrust of actual deal making. Yet no matter how many right moves you make, or however skilled you become at reading body language, building trust, framing arguments, or making offers or counter offers, success ultimately stems from good preparation. Careful preparation ensures you take the steps you need to be at the right table at the right time, with the right people and in possession of the right information. Far too many managers fondly believe they are great negotiators and enter these situations woefully underprepared.

Curiously, skilled and average negotiators tend to prepare for roughly the same amount of time. The difference lies in how each uses time. Average performers spend most of their preparation gathering data and massaging the numbers. In contrast, skilled negotiators devote most of their time to detective work, exploring soft issues and strategy, and deducing what the numbers tell them.

Good preparation means defining the answers to questions such as:

◆ What do we want from this negotiation?

◆ What would be our ideal outcome?

◆ What would an acceptable outcome?

◆ What is an unacceptable result – when would we walk away?

◆ What are our negotiating strengths and weaknesses and what are theirs?

What do successful negotiators need?

◆ A quick mind

◆ A strong reserve of patience

◆ The capacity to conceal without lying

◆ To inspire trust

◆ To realise when to be assertive and when to be self-effacing

◆ Knowledge of the issue

◆ The ability to see the bigger picture

◆ To ask plenty of questions

◆ To stick to one of two strong arguments, not many supporting ones

---

In high-stakes poker, the top professionals like to look as if they have just turned up. In fact, the best of them prepare meticulously for the event. Entering management negotiation with the above issues clear in your mind allows you to arrive at the table, like a professional poker player, with confidence and in possession of important knowledge.

To experience the full horrors of inadequate preparation, try negotiating with a skilled trade unionist. They usually receive in-depth training and if you find yourself in this territory, it could be well worth investing in some suitable off-site learning for yourself.

try negotiating with a skilled trade unionist

Assess your bargaining power

There was little room to negotiate with Mongol chieftain Genghis Khan. It got nasty and violent if you tried. When most of the power resides with the other side, there is little scope to bargain. Solving the mystery of how much bargaining power you possess may require all your detection skills, and be a critical factor in achieving a successful deal.

Experienced negotiators also constantly seek ways to strengthen their bargaining power or to weaken that of the other party. Naturally, your bargaining power influences the kind of outcome you can expect:

◆ win/lose – you gain but the other party loses

◆ win/win – you both gain a mutual benefit

◆ lose/lose – neither party gains a benefit.

These all assume the result is like a cake, fixed in size. Negotiation comes down to fighting for one's rightful share. Nowadays though, a more sophisticated approach assumes the cake can be both expanded and divided.

Game theory, which uses advanced maths, can sometimes help with the detective work of assessing power and potential outcomes by providing insight into how rational people behave when negotiating. However, newer approaches no longer assume rational behaviour.

Despite all the complexity of outcomes available, the best negotiators are those who prefer using their power to achieve a result that leaves everyone feeling good about it.

Adopt successful habits

What skilled negotiators do more of	What skilled negotiators do less of
◆ Check they have understood the other side – 'Let's recap on where we are.'	◆ Give information – 'Did you know...?'
◆ Ask for reasons – 'Can you justify that?'	◆ Acknowledge the person or their point – 'Yes quite, but as I was saying...'
◆ Ask for terms – 'What would your ideal volume be?'	◆ Disagree or contradict – 'No, but...'
◆ Create doubt – 'Have you considered the implications for...?'	◆ Make assumptions – 'I take it then that...'

Habit 1

Always know at what point you would be willing to walk away from the table. With this clear in your mind, you will feel a natural confidence about bargaining.

Habit 2

Be sure to include your highest value player. You cannot negotiate well in the absence of the person, organisation or representative who would get the best from the deal.

Habit 3

Include the most influential players who can make a difference to whether the negotiation succeeds or fails. This is more than demanding to see the organ grinder rather than the monkey. Look carefully to identify whom you most need around the table from the other side, to give the best chance of success.

Habit 4

Set up the right no-deal situation. It may pay you to bring in other parties to bolster your no-deal option. For example, transforming a two-party discussion into more of an auction can change the psychology of the deal, as well as the competitive pressures.

Habit 5

Where you want someone else to negotiate on your behalf, make sure they have the right skills to win the best deal. For example, will the agent really bargain hard enough for you?

Habit 6

Keep it simple and minimise the number of different parties involved. Too many people can complicate a negotiation, making it unwieldy.

Habit 7

Keep asking 'Why?' Do not merely discuss what your counterpart wants, uncover *why* they want it. Skilled negotiators are question addicts, asking more than twice as many questions as less skilled ones ask.

Use persistence

Top negotiators may claim their success relies on one key reason. It could be their willingness to walk away from a deal, knowing exactly what they want, good preparation and so on. One sure-fire guideline and the title of an excellent book by Gavin Kennedy is *Everything is Negotiable*.

While there are some situations where no negotiations seem possible, these are rare. For example, the widely made claim that 'we won't talk to terrorists' often proves to be spurious. In search of a political solution in Northern Ireland, the Blair government secretly offered to meet masked IRA representatives, despite repeated claims to the contrary.

Having tried to close a deal and been rejected, is it the end of the road? Not necessarily. It may be that it is worth continuing to play detective, investigating possible solutions and a powerful question to pursue is: 'What will it take to reach an agreement, despite our present difficulties?'

Following a no-deal response, it may seem costly to continue negotiating. But if you are confused about *why* your deal fell apart, it could be even more expensive to abandon it. Instead, next time you apparently lose a deal and head for the door, stick around and continue playing detective. What you discover may prove surprising, and allow you to put the deal back on track.

Specialist negotiators

Working in the HR department of a large company, Brian Jones (not his real name) decided to use Maynard Leigh Associates to deliver a culture change programme. Under his company rules though, the detailed contractual arrangements became the responsibility of the procurement department. The in-house negotiations experts started playing hardball, exerting sustained pressure on Maynard Leigh over price and cancellation terms. Eventually the Maynard Leigh consultant complained to Brian of bullying. Brian who did not want to drive away his preferred supplier, found himself negotiating with the procurement department to adjust its approach to the deal.

Companies often rely on specialist negotiators, like procurement officers, to extract the best bargains. The rise of these experts reflects the realisation that poor negotiating by line managers may leave an organisation exposed to both wasteful costs and avoidable risks. However, even if you succeed in

companies often rely on specialist negotiators to extract the best bargains

delegating the bargaining job, you will seldom escape becoming involved in the issues associated with it. Make sure those who bargain on your behalf have both the skills and your interests at heart to do the best deal.

Ways to negotiate successfully

☐ *Infuse your negotiations with patience combined with persistence*

☐ *Do your homework thoroughly on the negotiation issue*

☐ *Use the six stages of negotiation (prepare, offer, clarify, bargain, close and implement) to enhance your preparations for a deal*

☐ *Research the position of the other party to uncover what they most want*

☐ *Establish:*
   - *ideal outcome*
   - *acceptable outcome*
   - *when you would definitely walk away from the negotiations*
   - *what is negotiable*
   - *what is non-negotiable*

☐ *Keep returning to the bigger picture into which your negotiations fit*

☐ *Use varied questions to shed light on the position of the other party*

☐ *Rely on one or two strong arguments to support your position, rather than many*

☐ *Even if eventually you cannot achieve it, aim for a win/win situation*

☐ *Keep searching for common ground as a route to a deal*

☐ *Explore the alternatives to doing a deal*

13

Manage problem people

'TWO MOANS AND YOU'RE OUT' became the policy at IT specialist Nutzwerk after a successful anti-moaning campaign. 'If you are negative at Eden, you are fired,' CEO and co-founder of the Eden Project, Tim Smit says. 'Negative people are a cancer in the creative workplace.' Moaners can indeed be toxic and are just some of the types of problem people you may encounter and need to manage.

What seems a problem person though, may only be someone making your life difficult, for instance, by challenging your judgements, questioning your decisions, continually demanding explanations. Such behaviour may be awkward, yet may also be productive.

It can be dangerous branding someone as a problem person. First, they may just be different. Every organisation needs its mavericks. These people think counterintuitively, seeing the world in unexpected ways. Despite their problematic behaviour, they can be a vital source of new ideas, defining the

every organisation needs its mavericks

future or solving previously intractable problems. Secondly, problem people may be good at their job, despite their unwanted behaviour. They may simply have temporary difficulties and need your support, not punishment or the sack. Thirdly, by naming someone a problem person you potentially create a scapegoat who becomes an unwilling magnet for all kinds of blame. Not only may this be unfair it may eventually lead to an expensive claim for discrimination damages.

No one comes to work in order to fail. Start by assuming you have no problem people, only ones with problems, being in the wrong job, managed incorrectly or facing temporary difficulties. This is your chance to show you can get the best from people.

Even experienced managers sometimes admit, 'I've run out of ideas on how to deal with him,' or, 'She could do so much better but nothing seems to work,' or 'He simply can't follow instructions.' Many feel stressed over dealing with their difficult people.

Since under the right circumstances problem people can often be highly effective, try viewing their behaviour not as a problem but as a symptom. You need to alter behaviour, not their personality.

Confronted about their problem employees, senior managers sometimes confess the issue has been around for years. They simply never got round to resolving it. By tolerating poor behaviour and underperformance, you make it harder to manage the rest of your people who naturally draw conclusions about the acceptance of adverse behaviour. Rather than allow adverse behaviour to drift on for weeks or even months, take action. (See Chapter 10.)

Problem people

◆ Low fliers – sloppy or slow workers;
procrastinators; latecomers.

◆ Power players – abrasive toughies, or people who are
insensitive, loud or confrontational; prima donnas who
throw a tantrum until they get what they want.

◆ Whiners* – moaners who are perpetually finding fault;
pessimists with hundreds of reasons why things can't be
done; 'victims', who complain of unfair treatment.

◆ Deceivers – political players; those who manoeuvre
around the rules; gossips who spread
misrepresentations; resisters with out of control
habits such as drinking.

◆ Bullies – these get what they want through using excessive confrontation, conflict and a disregard for the views
and feelings of others.

◆ Liars – these distort information, manipulate and leave a
trail of distrust and, for example, undermine effective
team work.

◆ Worriers – overanxious individuals who instead of
turning their anxieties into useful behaviour, such as
attention to detail, demand constant attention and
reassurance.

*HR experts say these are the hardest to deal with.

Put it in perspective

Inexperienced managers or ones with a short fuse may rapidly conclude someone is a problem person and demand: 'I

want them off the bus – now!' This may be a sensible decision, but start by assuming the person needs support, not punishment. Before concluding you really have a problem person on your hands, raise your awareness about the nature of the behaviour. For example, how serious, frequent or entrenched is the behaviour, and what is the overall context of the problem? Only through awareness can you expect to develop your insight to arrive at practical solutions.

How serious?

Being around annoying, irritating or distracting people can be a pain. Yet how damaging is their behaviour? Does it affect other people's performance? Are they undermining your reputation or the team's? Do they lose the company money, customers or customer's respect? Put their actions in a larger perspective and decide whether it warrants any action at all.

How frequent?

Binge drinking twice a week may start to affect someone's work performance or endanger their health. If it occurs once a year celebrating a team success, it hardly warrants remedial action. Examine the facts about frequency. With a high-performer for instance, it may not be worth devoting time and energy to tackling occasional lapses.

How deeply entrenched?

You do not have time to tackle deep-seated behavioural problems, such as phobias or other forms of psychological disturbance. You may only be able to discover whether behaviour is deeply entrenched by holding one or more performance review sessions. (See Chapter 10.) If necessary, refer the person to other experts, such as therapists or specialist coaches.

Do we fully understand the context of this problem?

Make or obtain a detailed description of where the adverse behaviour happens and under what circumstances. When you come to examine the facts, you may conclude the person is reacting to particular kinds of situations where they feel under threat, out of their depth, or in response to excessive demands made on them.

Major change programmes, for instance, can unsettle people so much that they start showing resistance or behaving in unexpected ways. These symptoms may fade away once the change effort has taken hold.

Define it

Describe adverse behaviour with actual examples. It is not enough to know someone constantly arrives late to meetings. Back it up with dates, times and places. Solid facts about a problem help you become clearer about suitable action. For example, is the cause internal to the person or external?

- **Internal factors** – these are internal to the person such as poor motivation, hates meetings, poor time-keeping, low morale, bored, low drive, lacks ideas, impatient, poor concentration.

- **External factors** – these impinge on the person, such as over-long meetings, tired from overwork, seldom asked for an opinion, excessive workload, unwell, long commute, family problems, being bullied, suffering prejudice or discrimination.

By separating out and identifying these two factors, you will be a long way towards knowing how best to help this employee change.

Modifying behaviour

there is a whole kit bag of tools for tackling adverse behaviour

You do not need to be a therapist or brain surgeon to alter someone's problem behaviour. There is a whole kit bag of tools for tackling adverse behaviour including counselling, performance reviews, training, confrontation, job restructuring, transfers, punishment and dismissal.

One of the most effective managerial tools is behaviour modification (BM), which has nothing to do with brain washing or other dubious practices. BM influences people's behaviour using ideas from psychological research and practical experience. Using it, you ignore possible causes, focusing instead on direct action to influence behaviour. It aims to:

◆ affect the triggers that set off someone's behaviour, or

◆ reward the results of positive behaviours.

If you can discover what sets off someone's adverse behaviour you can try to alter or eliminate this factor. For instance, by continually warning someone to produce their reports on time you may merely be triggering their resistance to delivering in the first place. Rewarding is the second way to alter behaviour. For example, a team member may constantly interrupt because they realise it gains them attention. Or they learn through experience that it pays to use rudeness to avoid some task or responsibility.

Change the reward they get from their adverse behaviour and you begin affecting their actions. Rewards come in many guises, so do not think solely in terms of money. Praise, for instance, can be far more important. Punishment, a negative form of reward, can also affect behaviour. However, it tends to have unpredictable consequences and usually proves to be a poor way to manage. You quickly run out of options by relying on punishment to try to alter behaviour.

Reinforcement

Catch them doing something right and reward it. This long-standing BM approach helps you strengthen behaviour in the right direction and weaken adverse behaviours. For example, if you smile each time someone you manage says 'good morning' you will be positively reinforcing this behaviour and they are likely to repeat it. Similarly, by constantly tolerating persistent lateness in meetings and welcoming latecomers with a full summary of what has happened so far, you reinforce their adverse behaviour and they have every reason to continue it.

Reinforcement works best through encouraging small steps towards the final behaviour your want. You do not necessarily shoot for the moon immediately. Instead, you look for signs, no matter how small, that someone is changing in the right direction and reinforce these.

Suppose someone repeatedly delivers work several days late. After drawing attention to this and making sure there are no external factors to consider, you ask for an improvement. If the person delivers their work only slightly late next time, you reinforce this with encouragement, not another complaint. You might say for instance: *'Well done, I know this must have been quite an effort and I really appreciate how hard you have tried to deliver it on time. This really helps me with my own deadlines.'*

Modifying behaviour

Step 1:   Decide what the new behaviour needs to be: for example, arrives on time for team meetings and fully prepared.

Step 2:   Break down the change needed into smaller behavioural changes needed to reach the overall change. For example:

- ◆ still arrives late but much less than last time
- ◆ arrives hardly late but still unprepared
- ◆ arrives on time but still unprepared
- ◆ arrives on time and shows signs of doing some preparation
- ◆ arrives early and is fully prepared.

Step 3:   Watch for *any* behaviour moving in the direction of the first new behaviour. No matter how tentative the sign, describe it to the person, and offer support, encouragement and recognition; explain how it helps, for example, *'When you clearly try to arrive on time, this really helps the team meeting get off to a good start.'*

Step 4: Continue reinforcing the new behaviour; that is, encouraging or rewarding, whenever the behaviour occurs until it seems permanent.

Step 5: Now watch for any signs that behaviour is moving in the desired direction of the next step and reinforce/reward.

Confrontation

In tackling the problem person are you worried about making an unpleasant scene? Would you rather do almost anything to avoid such a scene? Even experienced managers sometimes duck a confrontation for fear of damaging a relationship or being unable to handle a colleague becoming emotional. Yet confrontation need not always be a miserable experience; it can be satisfying and inspiring. With confrontation you tackle adverse behaviour as it occurs or shortly afterwards. For example, you might establish a team rule that if someone behaves badly you will treat it like a speeding fine, tackling it within two weeks or not at all.

Promptness prevents resentment building to undermine respect and trust. Before it becomes deep-rooted, use regular development sessions to confront and uncover potentially troublesome behaviour. For example, you might ask team members to sit opposite each other in pairs and in five minutes discuss:

◆ 'What I really appreciate about you is...'

◆ 'What I want less of from you is....'

'I' statements

Although being a manager means you constantly use 'we' rather than 'I', when you confront someone over their problem behaviour it is usually best to use an 'I' statement, which makes it clear you are speaking for yourself, rather than other people. This makes the issue more real for the other person:

◆ *'I want you to pay attention during our meetings when someone else has the floor and is talking.'*

◆ *'I need this room to be really tidy by the time the MD arrives tomorrow.'*

Avoid indirect statements such as 'the team feels...', 'the company would like...' or 'it's not the done thing round here'. Positive confrontation consists of saying what you want, rather than what you do *not* want:

◆ rather than: *'Please stop talking to colleagues while I am briefing the team'*

◆ use instead: *'I want your full attention while I am briefing the team'.*

Confrontation often works best when based on careful preparation, rather than plunging in immediately without marshalling the evidence or planning your strategy.

it may be better to hold back

Commonsense tells you to stay calm and not lose your temper with the problem person, but this hardly helps in knowing how to tackle the situation. Rather than confront on the spot when the adverse behaviour occurs, it may be better to hold back and arrange the encounter for a time of your own choosing.

Managing a confrontation

In response to a disruptive team member:

◆ Gather evidence about how the rest of the team feels about the behaviour.

◆ Invite the person concerned to meet you in your office, in private.

◆ Describe the adverse effects of their behaviour on colleagues. Do not use 'team members feel this or that...' but practical examples, with your conclusions about the effects:

– 'I notice you keep interrupting at team meetings, and I see some members feeling angry with you.'
– 'When you rudely criticised Peter in the meeting not only did it upset him but it affected others in that way too.'

◆ Ask them to explain why they behave in this way.

◆ Invite them to behave differently next time.

◆ Explore ways in which they might alter their behaviour in the future. For example, 'Try using your sense of humour to see the funny side of someone being stupid in the meeting.'

Mediation

Mediation can resolve many difficult workplace conflicts between people and some managers become highly skilled at it. It helps create more adult-to-adult relationships in all areas of work. Royal Mail, for example, uses a mix of internal and external mediators.

A core part of the mediation skill is awareness that a conflict exists and would benefit from mediation. This might take the form of helping the people concerned tell others how they feel about some disagreement or situation. As you need confidence to handle a mediation situation it may be worth seeking some training in this area.

Sack em!

This is the nuclear option and many would argue a sign of ultimate managerial failure. Dismissal is seldom a pleasant task, even when the person has been troublesome for a long time. Also, employment legislation makes it essential to avoid this option if possible. At some point in your management career though you will be stuck with a problem person whose behaviour seems unmanageable. If you decide on dismissal, seek professional advice on how best to go about this since it is difficult terrain and can be costly if handled badly.

It is essential to reduce the possibility of legal action with sound documentation, such as up-to-date recorded warnings, and specific failures to perform described in terms of time and place. Dismissal can be a lengthy process, particularly in large organisations where advisers such as HR specialists and lawyers ensure you have jumped through all the right hoops in sequence.

Finally, do not take the process to heart. While it is no minor matter to sack someone, it does not have to be personally destructive for you either.

Ways to deal with problem people

☐ *Take control of the situation, not the person*

☐ *Head off trouble before it can turn into a disaster*

☐ *Learn to read behaviour, so you can objectively describe what is happening*

☐ *Separate internal factors causing behaviour problems from external ones*

☐ *Aim to leave the person feeling you want to help them, not punish or reprimand them*

☐ *Avoid using attitude as your definition of the problem*

☐ *Get beyond the label to more objective factors such as rudeness, lateness, lack of professionalism or failure to cooperate*

☐ *Consider how frequent, serious and entrenched their adverse behaviour is – is it worth tackling?*

☐ *Aim to alter behaviour, not their personality*

☐ *Confront seriously adverse behaviour immediately, do not let things drift*

☐ *Understand the context, not just the personality*

☐ *Effective confrontation starts with an 'I' statement about what you want*

☐ *Seek professional advice if you go for dismissal*

PART 3

Manage the organisation

SELF

OTHERS

ORGANISATION

Organisation

◆ Manage time and goals
◆ Manage change
◆ Make decisions
◆ Inspire meetings
◆ Encourage creativity and innovation
◆ Select and recruit
◆ Persuade and influence

Managing the organisation is being aware of the situation, realising the impact you want to make or could make, and how to make it. The seven management processes require you hone your awareness and insight so you can affect not just those you manage but a much wider constituency. Can you imagine working in a commercial organisation where everyone around you is a volunteer? To get anything done you would probably have to negotiate, persuade, wheel and deal. At any time, your army of volunteers could instantly choose to direct their energies elsewhere.

This is not quite the bizarre scenario it seems. Knowledge workers are now central to how many organisations operate and they do not take kindly to old-style management and leadership based on hierarchy, low trust and control. As Gary Hamel, international guru on management argues, such old ways of making things happen 'sit uneasily against a paradigm of volunteer knowledge workers who are expected to be accountable and empowered, willing and able to create shared learning and intellectual capital'.

If the environment proves unpalatable many experts and specialists can literally vote with their feet. Indeed entire teams of financial specialists, for example, regularly jump ship when tempted by better conditions or other inducements. Your interactions with the organisation are therefore an important aspect of surviving and thriving as a manager.

This third part deals with seven of the most critical aspects of managing the organisation: manage time and goals, manage change, make decisions, inspire meetings, encourage creativity and innovation, select and recruit, and finally persuade and influence.

14

Manage time and goals

THE AWESOME ATOM SMASHER AT CERN in Switzerland is the single largest, most complex engineering project in human history. This noble and inspiring undertaking cost billions, took 20 years of planning and construction by over 10,000 scientists from 85 countries. Their declared goal is to make a breakthrough in fundamental physics, something not achieved for quarter of a century. By contrast, only the vaguest goal existed for the construction of the London entertainment venue O_2. Consequently, the expensive Thames-side venue languished virtually unused for years, until a new owner arrived with a clear aim of how to make it a success.

Poorly chosen, badly defined or absent goals explain why individuals, teams, major projects and even entire companies sometimes go seriously astray. To thrive as a manager, develop your understanding and ability to select goals. The ones you choose will affect how you and other people use time and energy.

even entire companies sometimes go seriously astray

Setting goals

A widely used method for setting goals is the SMART method. These are goals that are: **S**tretching, **M**easurable, **A**cceptable, **R**ecorded and **T**ime-limited. (In earlier versions, the **S** stood for 'specific', but this is now incorporated within the Measurable goal.)

Stretching

People generally respond best to stretching or challenging goals, ones that put them on their mettle, giving them something for which to strive. Equally, over-ambitious goals cause trouble and can takes years to remedy. The US telecommunications company Lucent, for instance, had serious problems because 'we tried to grow our company faster than in hindsight it was able to do' (as reported in the *Financial Times*, 9 February 2001).

You may not always know whether people can achieve a stretching goal, until they get there.

Measurable

When Boeing decided to launch the 727 airliner it could have chosen the goal of building 'the best passenger plane in the world'. However, it needed a measurable goal, around which thousands of engineers and designers could coalesce. Boeing chose the SMART goal of building a plane to a strict timetable, to seat 131 passengers, fly non-stop from Miami to New York City, and land at LaGuardia's particularly short runway 4-22 of less than a mile.

Successful managers learn how to set ambitious long-term targets that also enable them to answer the question: 'How will we know when we have reached this goal?' For example, the desire to 'increase annual sales significantly' is an aspiration that, like the Boeing airliner, needs to be made concrete, such as 'by how much?' and 'when?'

Not all goals though, lend themselves to strict metrics and trying to make them measurable can be like chasing a phantom. Soft areas like the quality of client relationships or positive client feedback may not always respond to strict targets.

Some measurable goals may even become counter-productive, as happened at Rentokil. The CEO publicly admitted to spending years trying to abandon his self-imposed goal of always increasing annual earnings by 20 per cent. This unrealistic aim implied the entire country would end up working for the company (*Financial Times*, 2 February 2001).

Acceptable

Hercules famously struggled to complete the 12 labours set by the hated King Eurystheus, who had stolen his birthright. Had the king been able to consult a modern psychologist, he would have discovered that telling Hercules to set his own hard goals would have been smarter. People normally choose far more challenging goals for themselves than ones set for them by others. In fact, you may need to guide your people towards goals that, while acceptable, are also probably achievable.

Try initially presenting the goal you want your people to reach as a broad intention, allowing them time to explore it. For example, Motorola senior managers suggested to its engineers the ideal of producing a new range of mobile phones with virtually no rejects. Initially balking at this aspiration, natural curiosity took over. The sceptical engineers began asking how they might achieve zero defects and accepted the goal, eventually creating a production line with almost no failures.

Strike a balance between acceptable and tough goals. Think of it as a see-saw with tough at one end and acceptable at the other.

Make the goal too difficult and people may become disillusioned, unable to give it their wholehearted commitment. Make it too easy and it may not prove challenging enough. Choose a goal that does not tilt the see-saw too far in either direction.

Mandatory goals: Like Moses bringing tablets from the mountain, you may sometimes acquire goals from senior colleagues that you must take back and sell to your team or other colleagues. These mandatory goals may be essential to minimise uncertainty, deal with a crisis or simplify communications.

Presenting goals as non-negotiable may win reluctant compliance but no real commitment. You will first have to inspire people in some way, beginning by explaining why the goal is worth reaching for and why it is non-negotiable. Think of a time when someone has told you to do something and left you no real choice. It could have been a boss at work or some other voice of authority, including a teacher at school. How did the imposed goal make you feel? Did it inspire you and if so why? Or did it limit the chance to debate it, override conflict, and reduce personal autonomy and motivation rather than increase it? Goals arrived at through negotiation tend to be far more effective at switching on people's energy and enthusiasm.

Imposed goals	Negotiated goals
Limit debate	Encourage creativity
Minimise uncertainty	Promote participation
Override conflicts	Gain commitment
Useful in a crisis	Develop trust
Simplify communications	Encourage responsibility
Reflect management priorities	Expand individual influence
Inspire or challenge	Value people
Reduce personal autonomy	Promote personal autonomy

Recorded

While you can probably retain an important goal in your head, unless you are one of those rare people with total recall, it becomes harder tracking several dozen. If you manage many people, each striving towards a series of goals, you need to document these in some way. Recording can be as simple as listing goals in a notebook. Some easy-to-use IT systems document and monitor progress, particularly for large projects involving many sub-goals. Yet some of the best ways to track goals are by using simple visuals, screens or wall charts.

Putting goals on display for all to see can energise people, but only if they have signed up to them in the first place. Otherwise, they become mere slogans.

Time-limited

No date, no goal. Time limits provide a sense of urgency by clarifying expectations and, if necessary, people can change pace. A strict time limit for achieving a goal makes sense only if people know they cannot easily ignore it. A deadline that keeps changing is soon dead in the water. Help your people understand the likely consequence of not working to the agreed time limits.

a deadline that keeps changing is soon dead in the water

Be alert to deadline obsession where the time boundary, instead of being liberating, becomes a tyranny. When circumstances change, you need to be flexible enough to adjust either the goal or the time limit: for example, if you acquire a new manager who alters the direction of your department or budget cuts start to jeopardise growth projects.

What is your time worth?

'When employees know you respect their time they'll reward you with terrific performance,' argues the CEO of a major cosmetic company. 'When I see people waste time I call them on it immediately. Time is their greatest resource and when it's gone, it's lost forever.'

Make this simple calculation. Double your present salary figure and divide it by the number of hours in the year you work for the organisation. Doubling allows for overheads and below-the-line costs carried by your organisation. Exclude leisure time, such as thinking about work in the bath. Now calculate what you cost the organisation per hour. It can be shocking to realise how expensive you are. Keep reminding yourself of this hourly rate when making decisions about how to spend your time. Ask those who you manage to calculate their hourly rates too and discuss these with them.

Manage energy not time

What do you want to be remembered for? Presumably, not as that crazy manager who worked absurd hours making all their people miserable? When your children ask you to come to their school concert, don't you want to be there in the front row? Do you really want grudgingly to attend the parent–teacher events and be the one who keeps getting constant phone calls, tapping away frenetically on your Blackberry?

In fact, to be blunt, are you heading for an energy crisis? UK managers, for example, verge on being workaholics with most doing far more than their contracted hours. Rather than demonstrating efficiency, this culture of excess suggests the reverse and weak time management. It also creates low morale, limits exercise time and offers little scope to develop new skills.

You have a store of physical, emotional, mental and spiritual energy. Unlike time, you can revitalise each of these. If there is a single secret of time management beyond choosing

SMART goals, it is being assertive about managing personal energy. This can mean making sure you and your colleagues get enough sleep, take regular exercise and look after health and well-being. Deciding how you and they spend the day based on energy levels can transform everyone's approach to time management.

Misusing energy

Several hidden factors may lead to misusing your energy and that of others.

Judgement

If you do not trust your own judgement, you will end up doing what you assume everyone else wants you to do. Develop your natural assertiveness and ability to say 'no'. Learn to trust your instinct about how best to allocate your available energy.

Fragmentation

Studies of how managers spend their time reveal that most fritter it away, despite well-defined projects, goals and the essential knowledge to get the job done. Do not fragment your day and, instead, set priorities for distributing your energy and stick to them. People who set boundaries and priorities achieve far more than those who do not.

Feeling important

New managers particularly enjoy the clamour for their time. To beat the habit of constantly being busy you may need to overcome a deep desire to feel indispensible.

Urgency versus importance

The urgency and importance grid can help make sense of choices about how to use your energy.

Urgency/importance grid

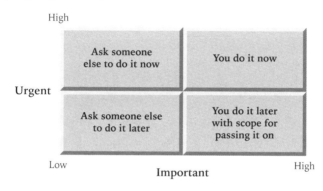

The best use of your time and energy will almost certainly be helping others manage theirs. Occasionally, though, there will be tasks you cannot allow to go wrong, such as potentially career-limiting issues that justify your full involvement. Anything seemingly both highly urgent and important probably warrants your energy spent on it, now. You can usually pass less significant issues to others.

To-do list

The humble, daily to-do list explains the secret of many managers' success at organising time, energy and goals. Whether you rely on a notepad, hand-held device, or some other system, the important thing is keeping a list of important tasks and using it daily.

No matter how hard you work, you cannot handle dozens of different tasks. Limit your daily list to 10 items and take a close look if it expands beyond that. Will the extra items:

◆ add value to the company

◆ be a creative contribution

◆ help others to be more effective

◆ help move towards a key target?

What can you do with uncompleted items? Moving them to the next day will soon clog up your daily list or become another list entirely. Instead, either drop the item or return it to a master list that tracks all your commitment and intentions.

Cut the clutter

While a tidy desk does not always indicate a tidy mind, you will focus on key goals better if not surrounded by disorder. Clutter not only messes with your mind, it makes you *feel* disorganised. It also sends a negative, 'I am overwhelmed' message to those you deal with. Some people use clutter as a way of saying 'Look how busy I am' or 'Help, I am not coping'. Be wary of letting this happen to you or those who report to you. If people feel overwhelmed it is important they can say so, and not do it by way of clutter.

Clutter can be physical, such as files, folders and paperwork but equally it can be an e-mail in-box bursting with hundreds of messages, unscheduled phone calls or constant interruptions.

The two secrets for dealing with physical paperwork are get rid of anything that looks like a pending tray, and aim to handle physical documentation just once.

Pending trays pile on the pressure. As material accumulates, it sits there accusingly. Start figuring out why you need a pending tray. Figure out how to eliminate it. For example, you might ask someone else to look after this material for you.

pending trays pile on the pressure

Phone madness

Mobiles persuade many of us we need to be constantly on call. This is a guaranteed waste of time and energy, since it puts you entirely at the mercy of other people who decide when to interrupt you. Rather than passively answering whenever your phone rings, fix specific times when you will be available and when you will not, and make this clear to people.

Try the following phone time savers.

◆ Rather than calling randomly, group calls you need to make into a fixed time slot.

◆ Avoid playing phone tag with those you want to reach. Suggest a time to talk, then be at your desk or free to talk on your mobile.

◆ Never leave a message on answering machines asking the person to call you back. This hands them the initiative, while you sit waiting powerless.

◆ Receiving constant text messages may give the illusion you are in the swim. Few, if any, will be critical. Rather than reading them whenever they arrive, check only every few hours.

E-mail madness

E-mails can become addictive, distorting how otherwise effective people use their energy. Some firms help their people deal with the daily avalanche in their in-boxes, hire e-mail consultants, and experiment with e-mail-free days. Google even uses an automatic lock out, forcing e-mail addicts to take a break from the screen.

Hundred of e-mails make you neither important nor truly informed. Count how many *significant* ones you receive on average each day. If there are more than about a dozen, start being proactive.

- Select someone to screen the incoming flood.
- Train your team to limit use of the Reply All button.
- Avoid multiple e-mail addresses.
- Remove yourself from voluntary distribution lists.
- Use only a few e-mail folders.
- Be ruthless, do not expect to read all your messages.
- Set up filters to group different priority e-mails, or by subject headings so you only read recent updates in a thread.
- Invest in a spam filter and do not open up the e-mails it collects, this merely encourages more to arrive.
- Avoid printing out e-mails: this is expensive, uses resources and is a waste of time.

City accountants Deloitte experimented with making Wednesday a day free of e-mails. The weekly amount of internal mail dropped as people became more conscious of what they were sending.

As a last resort, set your e-mail system to reject all e-mails that copy you in but do not address you specifically. This is a great idea, and you would love to do it, if only you weren't so pushed for time!

Ways to manage time and goals

☐ *Use SMART Goals: **S**tretching, **M**easurable, **A**cceptable, **R**ecorded and **T**ime-limited*

☐ *Establish how much you really cost your organisation per hour*

☐ *Manage your energy not time*

☐ *Be assertive in saying 'no' to wasteful demands on your time*

☐ *Take regular breaks to renew your energy*

☐ *Trust your judgement and make decisions*

☐ *Set priorities for how you will distribute your energy and stick to them*

☐ *Resist the siren call to feel indispensible*

☐ *Use the urgency and importance grid to decide on who does what*

☐ *Keep a current to-do list with no more than about 10 items per day*

☐ *Cut the clutter: banish anything looking like a pending tray*

☐ *Aim to handle all physical documentation just once*

☐ *Establish reliable and regular monitoring systems to tell you what is happening against the agreed timetable*

☐ *Organise your use of the phone and use phone savers*

☐ *Rationalise your e-mails, for example only seeing items directly addressed to you, not ones where you are merely copied in*

15

Manage change

HAVE YOU EVER BEEN WHITE WATER RAFTING? If not, you have probably caught TV scenes of helmeted, thrill-seekers battling the currents, steering their vulnerable craft over rapids and away from dangerous rocks and reefs. Managing change in organisations is rather like that. Once you become a manager, you automatically join the boat crew, and may even sometimes be the captain. With change pervasive and constantly accelerating, you could just sit back in your office and let nature take its course. But as with white water rafting, even when the currents seem benign, it seldom makes sense to abandon your fate to them.

Successful managers become change agents. They learn to deal with it even if, like the white water rafter, they cannot entirely control either the speed or direction of the journey. Going with the flow may seem an easy option, yet can make you entirely reactive, so you feel out of control of the swirling changes happening around you.

Being a change agent mainly concerns tackling organisational shifts, rather than altering a specific person's behaviours. At a personal level, it challenges you to live with uncertainty, tolerate ambiguity and avoid becoming dangerously risk averse. Managing change is tough and studies show that in most organisations two out of three attempts fail. The more things change the more they stay the same.

avoid becoming dangerously risk averse

The organic view

In an ant colony, there is no boss sending out orders, yet important decisions still emerge. A river never agonises about where to flow, yet still the water finds its own level. These are complex adaptive systems, offering important lessons for anyone attempting to create change in a human organisation.

Like the ant colony or a river, companies and people are also complex adaptive systems. That is, even with intensive study they are largely unpredictable. Simple rules of cause and effect do not necessarily apply. Foreseeing the outcome from a particular change will nearly always be hit and miss.

This organic view differs from treating the organisation as a machine, where pulling a particular lever will produce a known effect. An organic approach to change may seem wildly removed from the world of management. Yet taking it can prevent you from making wrong assumptions or having unreal expectations about likely results of change programmes. For example, an organic approach to change means accepting that there will be uncertain results from most important decisions. Even so, the right choices will often emerge naturally.

Rather than relying on so-called rational decision making, with the organic perspective you allow creative solutions to surface naturally. With this approach, you steer change, rather than direct it.

Route maps

'You have reached your destination,' drones the robotic, schoolmistress voice of the on-board SatNav. It would be wonderful if these ubiquitous devices could also tell us how to reach our chosen destination regarding organisational change. Unfortunately, no one has yet invented a credible SatNav for organisational change, and there are over 6000 books on change and management, each with their own take on how best to do it.

Without a reliable SatNav for organisational change, you will need to evolve your own route map of how best to make it happen. The four signposts to plant along your way are as follows.

1 Treat change as a process, not as a one-off, single event.

2 Assess carefully how long the change will take to complete.

3 Be clear how many people will be needed to execute the change.

4 Clarify the financial benefits and cost of the proposed change.

Treating organisational change as a continuous process means you act more like someone at the tiller of a sailing boat, constantly making small adjustments and the occasional large one, than someone pressing a button.

Operational versus strategic

As a change agent, it helps if you distinguish between operational change and fundamental strategic change.

◆ **Operational change** consists of alterations in procedures or activities. Because these mainly deal with day-to-day matters, you give less attention to exploring or anticipating long-term implications.

◆ **Strategic change** deals with cultural, structural, market or process shifts. These will tend to have long-term implications for how the organisation functions and require both careful thought and detailed planning.

Apart from using this distinction, what else might appear on your mental route map of achieving organisational change? It might include these specific activities:

◆ develop a change strategy – setting out how you will get there

◆ use vision and values – applying 'big picture' thinking to where you want to go

◆ use personal leadership – showing people how to get there

◆ deal with conflict and resistance – overcoming blockages to change

◆ encourage fresh thinking – generating new perspectives about change

- obtain commitment – engaging people's enthusiasm and energy

- adopt project management – instilling ways to progress and monitoring the change process

- communicate – making sure all stakeholders know what they need to know

- make change stick – embedding the changes so old ways do not return.

Develop a change strategy

The simplest route map for organisational change explains your expected destination. It is a move from

here ————————➤ to ————————➤ **there**.

This may sound dangerously naive, yet more change efforts fail from lack of clarity about the intended destination than practically any other cause. (See also Chapter 14.)

By treating the planned change as a journey, not a desti-nation, you will almost naturally tend to break it into stages, without necessarily assuming there is an end.

Use vision and values

How did the struggling Co-operative bank of the 1990s become a more vibrant and effective organisation, well-positioned to succeed in the 21st century? Likewise, how did M&S, seemingly destined to fall into the maw of hungry predators, bounce back? Both organisations experienced a successful transformation. The Co-operative bank did it by building on its core values to create a modern and vibrant new culture. M&S returned to its core values of style and value for money, while shaking up a moribund organisation.

Values tell people how you want things to be – that is, what matters. They bind a team or an entire company together like a glue to give change programmes coherence. Talk, talk, talk the values! Your job as a change agent is first to articulate values, secondly to explain how to turn them into practical action, and finally to demonstrate them by your own behaviour. When you model the way, others will follow.

talk, talk, talk the values!

Apply personal leadership

As explained in Chapter 7, effective managers show leadership. In managing change, this means you step out there and describe the desired future. People need to see you thinking and acting strategically.

So, what are your organisation's aspirations and strategic intent? If you do not know, find out, even if this appears to be notionally outside your immediate area of responsibility. Do this by seeking answers to questions like:

◆ Where is this organisation going?

◆ Where can it or should it go?

◆ What are we ultimately trying to achieve (avoid simplistic answers like 'to make a profit' or 'world domination')?

◆ What is our corporate vision for the future?

Not all senior colleagues may welcome your enquiries, particularly if they themselves feel unsure of the answers. When people see you ask the questions though, it will certainly raise your profile, so long as you do it from a genuine sense of curiosity.

Handle conflict and resistance

'Resistance is futile' goes the famous line from the sinister Borg in the TV series *Star Trek*. Not only is resistance to change often not futile, it may be entirely rational. When Shell met strong staff reaction to dumping one of its oil rigs in the North Sea, the internal staff anger was entirely appropriate. Had the company leadership listened better, it would have avoided the damaging public reaction, which later forced a painful reversal.

Resistance to a change may conveniently happen in a low-key way. Equally, it may erupt into conflict, pitting one group against another, producing damaging splits across the organisation. Conflict invariably involves emotion and strong feelings. Consequently, conflict management is unavoidably part of the basic skills of any manager who aspires to be a successful change agent.

Practical actions include:

◆ bringing conflict to the surface rather than allowing it to fester

◆ working with those experiencing it to dissect and analyse what it is really about

◆ treating conflict as usually healthy, adding rigour to decisions

◆ acting as a mediator, nudging the parties to get closer or compromise

◆ controlling the escalation of tension by thinking ahead and nipping issues in the bud.

Are you comfortable with such a situation, or do you fervently wish to be anywhere else than in the eye of the storm? Consider using an external resource such as a specialist workshop on conflict resolution to boost your skills and confidence in this area.

Manage risk

From mastering the deadly sabretoothed tiger to facing up to climate change, human survival has always depended on dealing with risk. In fact, risk avoidance is a natural human instinct. Any organisational change effort you are involved in will come with some kind of risk attached to it. Part of your role as change agent will be making sense of the nature and extent of that risk.

If you manage IT systems, risk assessment is almost a profession in its own right. In organisational change, though, calculation of risk is nowhere near that level of sophistication. Therefore, what matters most is ensuring risk does not turn into recklessness. Reckless organisational change occurs when managers make unreasonable assumptions about the likely benefits or outcomes from a particular change initiative.

At the macro level, the poor record of success in mergers and acquisitions with few delivering their expected business benefits shows how risk can become reckless, destroying shareholder value and achieving little practical benefit for years to come. At the micro level, even minor structural changes, such as who reports to whom or how certain types of projects will be handled can trigger all kinds of unexpected and sometimes destructive forces.

Assess the risks and, where possible, quantify them.

Obtain commitment

'It is a marathon, not a sprint,' say those familiar with organisational change efforts. Large-scale change seldom proves simple or quick. Effective change agents know their biggest challenge in new ways of working, behaving or thinking is winning people's commitment.

For the changes you want to make you will need to seek visible backing from the most influential people in your organisation, who may not necessarily hold the top titles. You also need to take into account the enthusiasm, or lack of it, of those who will deal with the new systems, processes or ways of working.

Who are the stakeholders affected by the change you have in mind? How will you gain their involvement? Stakeholders who will support or oppose the change will implicitly be asking, 'What's in it for me?' There is nothing particularly selfish or self-serving about this response. People only absorb the case for change by personalising it, relating it to themselves, to their own job, their team or even their family.

Decide whom you need to commit to the change, and how to involve them in the whole process.

Adopt project management

The soft side of change management gets plenty of attention. But the hard side matters too, focusing on detailed implementation and breaking the change effort into manageable projects.

Your project teams need clear goals with recognisable milestones, with regular reporting on progress. They also need to accept that anyone not directly involved in the change work has scope to increase their workload in the change cause by probably not more than 10 per cent. More than this and people will become overstretched and unable to support the change initiative.

choose your project leaders for their enthusiasm

Choose your project leaders for their enthusiasm for the change effort, not just because they are good technicians or competent professionals.

Communicate

'It's good to talk' went a famous BT advertising slogan and much the same applies to change programmes. Many start with a solid communication effort to explain what will happen and when. But far too many such efforts are more like product branding exercises than a continuous conversation between people. Without a continuous dialogue between those seeking change and those who must make it happen, people can soon feel out of touch. They wonder, for example, if the change effort is failing, or they lose the motivation to stay involved.

Build a continuous communications process into your change strategy. It may take varied forms, from regular town hall meetings to monthly newsletters, from e-mail updates to celebrations of reaching critical stages in the programme.

Be proactive in personally talking about the change programme, making yourself available to people who have concerns about it, or are responsible for some aspect of implementation. Find imaginative ways to remind staff of the overall case for change and to reinforce its benefits to them.

Make change stick

Any fool can launch a change programme. To make it stick though, demands a combination of awareness, insight and persistence. You need to become constantly aware of where you are in the programme and be ready to take action against inertia and a natural tendency to return to old patterns of behaviour.

Vary the ways you keep the momentum going. Your persistence agenda might include: publicity to reinforce the basic change message constantly; talks by change enthusiasts; celebrations; clever use of procedures and policies; small interactions over coffee or by the water cooler; mass e-mails; write-ups in the media or internal newsletters; and town hall type meetings.

Because most change efforts are a journey not a destination, you need to find champions for your change effort. Their job is to keep raising the profile of the programme by talking about it, encouraging action and using their influence to make an impact.

you need to find champions for your change effort

Ways to manage change

- [ ] *Develop your ability to tolerate ambiguity and uncertainty*
- [ ] *View your organisation as more like a living organism than a machine*
- [ ] *Master the differences between operational and strategic change*
- [ ] *Start to develop your own route map for managing the organisation's change*
- [ ] *View change efforts as a journey, not a destination*
- [ ] *Articulate values and explain how they will be turned into practical action*
- [ ] *Demonstrate change values through your own behaviour*
- [ ] *Build an engaging word picture of how the future should look*
- [ ] *Talk constantly about the change programme and show your enthusiasm for it*
- [ ] *Develop your capacity to think and act strategically*
- [ ] *Anticipate resistance to change with strategies for dealing with it*
- [ ] *Treat conflict as healthy, adding rigour to change decisions*
- [ ] *Practise thinking outside the box and encouraging others to do the same*
- [ ] *Identify who are the stakeholders affected by the change*
- [ ] *Discover the best people to be involved in implementation*

☐ *Break down the overall change into small, more-manageable chunks*

☐ *Use project teams to tackle chunks of the change effort*

☐ *Build a continuous communications process into your change strategy*

☐ *Establish regular monitoring systems to tell you what is happening*

☐ *Make change stick using persistence and by enrolling champions to promote it*

16

Make decisions

ASKED HOW SHE HAD MANAGED TO SUCCEED in such a male-dominated environment the first woman admiral in America, the formidable Grace Hopper, reportedly growled her secret for successful decision making: 'I guess you do it first, and apologise later.'

The detached and impassive executive may fit our mental picture of the ideal corporate decision maker, yet people actually make better choices when they experience intense emotions. Ignoring the emotional content of a decision can also prove costly.

British Airways changed the design of all its aircraft tail fins by dropping the Union Flag in favour of art from around the world. The company based its expensive repainting decision almost entirely on the numbers from consumer feedback. But a smaller group of highly-profitable and influential customers, who disliked the new design, eventually forced the airline to scrap it. The best decision makers embrace emotions and the use of intuition, without allowing these to lead them astray.

Making decisions is what managers are supposed to do. Real life can be very different. The number of decisions made by a new or relatively inexperienced manager is far less than the traditional image of a busy manager. So it is important that the ones you do make are as good as they can be.

making decisions is what managers are supposed to do

Only robots make decisions based entirely on numerical data. But a whole science of decision making uses complex models, subtle theories and clever systems for identifying options, attaching probabilities and assessing risk. Is that what the management job is really about, and does it mean you must master this discipline or risk being a failure?

'Often you have to rely on your intuition' remarked Microsoft's Bill Gates. This gets you closer to how the world actually works.

Satisficing

In studying those making high-stake choices, researchers initially assumed they would be rational, just like the decision models predict:

> *Gather information, identify possible solutions, choose the best ones, and evaluate the results.*

Their assumptions were wrong.

The evidence revealed people seldom bother with comparing difference choices. Instead, they merely find something better than their starting point. They commonly select *the first reasonable option they encounter* – an approach called satisficing. It happens because of time pressures, the low penalty for guessing wrong, or awareness that weighing many options may not improve the chances of success.

Most managerial decisions therefore emerge as satisficing, mixed with some effort at being a little more rational. Only when the stakes are truly exceptional is there usually some attempt to go beyond straight guessing.

Even using elaborate decision-making methods, you can seldom accurately predict all the consequences from a particular choice. You may have done the calculations, gathered all the available facts, studied and compared all the options yet the outcome still proves different to expectations. How else can one explain all those expensive failed mergers and acquisitions around the world?

All this suggests that you will be better with a rather different decision-making approach from the ultra-rational one usually thrust at new or inexperienced managers.

Essential decision-making behaviour

In a 1999 charity auction for life-sized, black and white fibre-glass cows intense rivalry surfaced for the artist-designed objects and over-bidding led to crazy prices for the cattle. It was a classic case of dangerous competitive arousal, which also affects managers when they go in single-minded pursuit of victory.

Rivalry, time pressures and being in the limelight may all reinforce each other to distort decision making. In fact, the brighter the spotlight, the greater potential for competitive arousal and bad decisions. Be alert to the potentially harmful dynamics of competitive arousal and make sure your decision making occurs in a more ordered way. Set out to defuse rivalry, reduce the time pressures and deflect the spotlight.

Intuition, as we have seen already, plays a vital role in most decision making. While intuition can seem magical, it mainly relies on using knowledge based on experience. When being intuitive you move knowledge from your unconscious to your conscious mind, which is why sleeping on it before finally deciding makes sense.

You do not learn intuitive decision making so much as tap into this human capacity with four steps:

1   Preparation – get some knowledge or experience.

2   Incubation – allow your mind time to ruminate over the choices.

3   Illumination – arrive at a realisation.

4   Verification – check the realisation using your rational mind.

Based on the above and the evidence from how managers actually make sound decisions the best approach is to:

◆   get fully involved in your decisions

◆   tap into and trust your emotions

◆   use your natural ability to reason.

Ego

When your job so clearly depends on making a good decision, why would anyone knowingly make a bad one? The choice has nothing to do with numbers or even lack of information. What often gets in the way is a misguided determination to make a mark by doing something dramatic. Many managers want to be remembered for having changed the company in a significant way.

When it comes to decision making, therefore, keep a close check on your ego – make choices because they are right for the organisation, not because they will impress others.

Involvement

Teams and groups often make collective decisions they would not have taken individually. This phenomenon, called group think, is both common and potentially dangerous. One well-known CEO regularly adjourned meetings where everyone seemed to be supporting a particular decision. He valued a diversity of opinion and insisted on another meeting 'to get some constructive disagreement going'.

Keep a watch for signs of group think, where everyone seems to agree, with concerted heads nodding, rather than a diversity of views. In the global consultancy Accenture, for example, an anti group think technique used in certain group discussions only allows people who disagree to speak, not those who agree.

On tap or on top?

Could the route to better decision making be to call in the experts to reinforce your opinions or make sense of complicated choices? It might just work, but this puts them on top, rather than on tap, and extensive research into the ability of experts to make predictions shows they suffer from an important deficiency: they fail to learn from experience. Curiously, only two expert groups seemed actively to learn from experience – weather forecasters and bridge players, mainly because they get instant feedback.

only two expert groups seemed actively to learn from experience

Since you will probably make only a few really important big decisions in your entire management career it could be years before your discover whether you made the right one. So learning from your mistakes may be of only limited use.

Without simply passing the entire decision-making task to an expert, a sound approach is to require a risk assessment. Here the use of experts may prove effective for exploring questions such as:

◆ How *big* is the risk we run with this choice?

◆ What is the likelihood or *probability* of a particular outcome occurring?

◆ How could we *reduce* or even eliminate the risk?

◆ What is the *worst-case* scenario?

Formal decision-making systems use risk in a particular way. Rather than concluding an outcome is uncertain, risk assessment tries to quantify the extent of this uncertainty – the chances of something happening. But while there may be all kinds of sophisticated probability calculations, ultimately the final assessment still comes down to an informed guess.

Proper risk analysis is therefore a numerate discipline involving applied mathematics and numerous statistical techniques. Few busy managers have time to become experts in it, which is why calling in an expert may sometimes prove to be justified.

Scenarios

Scenarios help make sense of tricky choices by systematically exploring what might happen if everything goes badly wrong. Using them often drains the decision situation of its mystery and ability to generate excessive fear.

What happens if we launch this product as planned?

- Worst-case scenario: it fails dramatically, costing large amounts of money and prestige.

- Best-case scenario: it succeeds beyond our wildest dreams.

- Most likely scenario: it goes reasonably well, providing a possibility for further investment.

What happens if I confront this person about their persistent lateness?

- Worst-case scenario: they become angry, storm out and file a case for constructive dismissal, bullying and discrimination.

- Best-case scenario: they acknowledge the problem and completely transform their timekeeping.

- Most likely scenario: they reluctantly agree it is an issue and start making noticeable improvements.

What happens if we discount to match the prices offered by our main competitor?

- Worst-case scenario: we start a price war which we lose, because we cannot match their resources; key customers defect and we suffer a large drop in profitability.

- Best-case scenario: we annihilate the opposition, attracting many of their best customers and put their whole strategy in doubt.

- Most likely scenario: no further reductions are made by either side and our market share remains unchanged; profitability gradually returns to normal.

Decision kit bag

Experienced decision makers gradually accumulate their own store of usable methods. Many include the earlier point about trusting gut instinct, while underpinning it with solid data.

Knowing the tools you might adopt in different situations will assist your decision making, enabling you to evolve your own kit bag of possible ways to make important choices.

The following box is not a definitive list and you do not need to master everything. However, discovering how and when each method could prove useful in your decision making. Do so either through further reading or by attending a decision-making workshop.

Decision kit bag

The following methods could help you in your decision making but don't get distracted by reams of numbers and analysis if the basic principles, assumptions or conclusions seem to defy common sense.

◆ **Statistical methods** are varied and include averages, dispersion, indices, time series, sampling, regression and probability distributions.

◆ **Decision models** simulate different situations, allowing you to alter the various parameters to see the possible outcomes. Many of the best models rely on using spreadsheets.

◆ **Linear programming** is a statistical technique that takes into account the various constraints affecting important choices.

◆ **Pareto analysis** is used for choosing the most effective changes to make.

◆ **Grid analysis** is used for making a choice involving many factors.

◆ **Decision tree analysis** provides a visual structure in which to lay out options and investigate possible outcomes.

◆ **Force field analysis** identifies forces to strengthen or weaken in attempting to make a particular decision work.

◆ **SWOT analysis** brings together a more holistic picture of the decision options through examining the Strengths, Weaknesses, Opportunities and Threats from different courses of action.

◆ **Cost-benefit appraisals** provide a systematic way of quantifying the likely costs and returns from a particular decision, often where actual numerical data is in short supply.

A fine distinction

Situational analysis offers one of the best approaches to rational decision making. It recognises important differences between a decision, a problem and a plan. Each has slightly different implications for how you approach them, what kind of information you gather and what action you take.

In situational analysis, a problem is something that has already occurred and a deviation from what you wanted or expected to happen. This does not require a decision so much as unravelling what happened and possible remedial action. Problems may eventually have simple solutions, but many involve so much complexity they may not have an easy answer or indeed any at all. By contrast, a plan shows the steps for reaching a particular goal in the future. It requires you to map out the route and anticipate problems along the way.

a plan shows the steps for reaching a particular goal in the future

Finally, a decision involves choices, and the need to generate and evaluate alternatives. Many managers have trained in situational analysis, often called the Kepner–Tregoe method.

Despite the natural tendency to satisfice (see above), there can be no real decision without some choices, even if they are never fully considered. With no viable alternatives then decision making becomes irrelevant. For example, if cleaning food counters must be to national standards of hygiene, there can be little sense debating alternatives.

Making it stick

Most decisions that go wrong do so not from careless analysis, insufficient alternatives, and lack of information or even bad judgement. The most common reasons are insufficient support across the organisation and failure to follow-through.

Making consistently sound decisions requires you to be open to alternative views by involving other people in the process. You need to know the truth about your impending decision but people must trust that you will not see them as negative or disloyal. You may need to find ingenious ways to ensure you hear frank opinions.

In the search for making the decision stick, consider asking:

◆ 'Whose help do I need to make it happen?'

◆ 'What do I need to gain their commitment?'

◆ 'Who could undermine or prevent this decision from being implemented?'

To help answer these questions it can be useful to generate a visual representation to show the relationships between the different stakeholders or influencers.

As you advance

Adapting your decision-making approach as you climb the career ladder may prove particularly challenging. In the early days, you may tend towards directive and command orientated approaches. Yet, as you progress, you will need to adopt a more open style that seeks diversity of opinion and participative decision making.

Research reveals that the most successful managers adapt their decision-making style, while the least successful stagnate because they continue to be directive while trying to be participative, action focused and open to alternatives. The higher you go, the further you get from front-line action and the easier it becomes to lose touch with what is happening in the organisation. Isolated decision making is a killer and explains why many top managers stumble, sometimes fatally.

Evolving how you make decisions so you can engage others in the process will therefore be an important factor in whether you thrive in your management career.

Ways to make decisions

☐ *Get fully involved in your decisions*

☐ *Tap into and trust your emotions*

☐ *Use your natural ability to reason*

☐ *Keep a close check on your ego, make choices that are right for the organisation, not because they will impress others*

☐ *Watch for signs of group think, rather than a diversity of views*

☐ *Consider bringing in an expert on risk assessment if the stakes are high*

☐ *Use scenarios to help make sense of tricky choices*

☐ *Become familiar with the main tools for decision making and what they can do*

☐ *Distinguish between a plan, a decision and a problem and how to approach them*

☐ *Consider who can help make your decisions stick, whose commitment you need and who could undermine them in some way*

☐ *As you progress adapt your decision-making style to be more open and inclusive*

17

Inspire meetings

THE AGENDA LOOKED MUCH THE SAME as usual with nothing special about date or time. But <u>Location</u>, underlined in red, jumped out from the rest of the page: 'We face a huge challenge this year and our meeting to discuss it starts beside the Colossus ride at Thorpe Park.'

The average manager attends several dozen meetings a month and far too many prove to be a waste of time.

- ◆ **Boredom:** nine out of ten admit to daydreaming during meetings and at least four confess to actually falling asleep.

- ◆ **Confusion:** uncertainty about what the meeting will achieve is common.

- ◆ **Conflict:** participants seem so busy settling old scores and winning arguments they never address the job in hand.

- ◆ **Ego:** one or two people grab the 'airtime', control the agenda and stop others contributing or getting a hearing.

You can tell an inspiring meeting when everyone feels stimulated to attend and leaves believing it has been worthwhile. Sometimes an unusual location, like the Colossus ride example, can bring a meeting alive. In such encounters, people may not always like what they hear, yet still come away uplifted by the experience and feeling it was worthwhile.

a reputation for running effective, inspiring meetings can enhance your career

A reputation for running effective, inspiring meetings can enhance your career. Despite the negative image of meetings as mainly unproductive places, you will probably get many things done through them. So it makes sense to become good at the various tasks involved: convening, preparing, chairing, participating and ensuring follow-up.

Some managers never master the art of running effective meetings and consequently damage their entire careers. Even if you dislike formal meetings, commit to trying to make them enjoyable and productive. Once people realise you nearly always call worthwhile meetings, with focus, pace and relevance, you will rapidly attract a good attendance.

Why bother?

Zero in on any meeting on your patch that keeps happening regularly and review whether it really is necessary. Ritualised sessions, such as a weekly team gathering, may feel reassuring yet can acquire a life of its own with people going through the motions and never really making anything happen.

Lack of focus is a sure way to create dud meetings. Multiple topics and heavy agendas may look impressive, but people soon feel overwhelmed and unsure of what they can achieve. To tighten up on purpose establish a single headline that sums up what the meeting is about. 'Before starting can we just clarify the purpose of this meeting?' This simple request can transform meetings riddled with vague intentions into something more concrete. Hearing the reply you may find occasionally that you can respond: 'In that case, I don't think I should be here,' and leave.

Once people detect your readiness to withdraw unless there is clarity of purpose, they tend to ensure it exists before inviting you. This is one way you can start affecting how the organisation handles its meetings.

Come prepared

Preparation remains the Achilles' heel of many managers. Never assume your mere presence justifies a meeting. Make time to prepare well: for example, read papers sent for discussion, talk to people in advance about the issues, collect information and begin formulating your views.

Once people realise you normally do your homework they will tend to listen more carefully, giving your views more weight. With good preparation, you will feel more confident to listen openly while being careful to show you have not already made up your mind.

Attendance

Devote time to ensuring the right people attend because their contribution will be essential or you need their commitment or involvement in some way. Also, watch out for meeting creep, where the number attending escalates through fear of offending certain people or from gatecrashers. Explain why you have chosen specific people to attend. 'I need you there because...' can prove a compelling incentive for people to turn up, even though they are extremely busy.

Manage the agenda

Whoever controls the agenda partly controls the meeting. This underrated skill can save countless wasted hours. Create written agendas, in advance or right at the start, allocating time according to urgency, importance and complexity.

Agendas tend to grow as people add items, many of which may be nice to discuss, yet are not essential. This does not mean excluding any time on pleasant or social discussion; just set some boundaries for this activity. For example, create a parking lot for issues you do not want to discuss now.

Clarify whether each agenda item is for

◆ information only

◆ discussion, or

◆ decision.

Be willing to break with tradition, eliminating long-serving items like any other business (AOB). These tempt people to drone on about their pet idea or even hijack the entire meeting. Invite those with new items to add them to the next agenda. Anything genuinely urgent will usually surface at the start as you seek to clarify the purpose of the gathering. Similarly, rather than the ritual of reading out

seek to clarify the purpose of the gathering

previous minutes, manage by exception, by checking in advance on previously agreed actions, allowing only those without known follow-through to surface.

Repeatedly carrying forward items not dealt with causes future agendas to spin out of control. Suggest items returned more than twice be dealt with in one of these ways:

◆ discussed immediately

◆ sent for attention elsewhere, or

◆ dropped entirely.

Good agenda habits

◆ Aim for a written agenda

◆ Distribute the agenda in advance

◆ Explain location, date, start and end times

◆ Make agenda creation a participative experience

◆ Agenda items should reach the chairperson well in advance of the meeting

◆ Start with easy items, put harder items in the middle, and end on an up note

◆ After each agenda item, summarise the main point, and state what the result/action will be, when it is to be completed, and by whom

---

Chairing

You do not need to lead every meeting you convene. Often it makes sense to let others do it, while you watch what goes on and play a supporting role. If others lead the session, ensure they acquire the necessary skills. Give them some help with what people expect from a good chairperson.

If you do chair the meeting, take responsibility for ensuring that everyone receives airtime, and make it clear you expect to hear from everyone.

Note taking and minutes

Whoever takes on this role needs to understand about action minutes. These simply record what the meeting agreed should happen next. Strongly resist discursive commentary about who said what at the meeting as this leads to lengthy minutes attempting to capture everything that occurred. When, however, multiple teams work on a project, it may be useful occasionally to show the reason for a decision or the context for some action.

Time keeping

Meetings that start and end promptly rapidly acquire a sound reputation. Keep reviewing the pace of the meeting so if the discussion drifts you can take action quickly. Invite everyone to help the meeting stay focused. You might even agree a group visual signal that people can use to suggest the discussion is heading off course.

Five minutes before the end, warn attendees of the amount of time left: it will help people refocus. Consider appointing someone to keep track of the time and to give feedback regularly on this aspect.

Late arrivals

These interrupt meetings and undermine good time keeping. Be willing to explain that you expect people to be punctual as a sign of respect for everyone's time.

Avoid confronting latecomers in public and never assume their behaviour stems from laziness or a desire to be awkward. Perhaps they have important care duties at home before leaving, face a particularly difficult commute or have some other solid reason. Privately enquire about the reasons as simply asking the question may result in them arriving on time in future. If someone keeps arriving late for no good reason, give them the role of meeting timekeeper. After doing this for a while they will naturally tend to arrive on time.

Are you inadvertently encouraging late arrivals? For instance, by always starting your meetings late to accommodate them, you punish the rest who arrived promptly. Similarly, by offering late arrivals a full summary of the discussion so far you punish the rest who must sit through it, and this rewards anti-social behaviour.

If normally late arrivals come on time, publically thank them; maybe even send a written note appreciating their effort. Give them a role too, such as ensuring the meeting stays on course. This shows you have renewed confidence in them. When late arrivals try to slip into the meeting unnoticed, stop the meeting and welcome them, but also tactfully invite them to apologise to everyone else if they do not offer one without prompting.

Two last-resort measures:

1   Ask a persistent late arrival not to attend, since this may be what they want in the first place, and be ready to do without them.

2   Publicise and effect a closed-door policy in which no one may enter once the meeting starts. Excluded in this way, people almost always arrive promptly next time.

Finally, get tough about timing and most people will welcome it.

Control the environment

Many meetings happen informally in a coffee area or casually in the corridor in which case you cannot do much about the environment. But for formal meetings make sure the environment contributes to an effective experience. For instance, are there avoidable distractions such as stunning views outside, poor lighting, uncomfortable seating or refreshments due to arrive at the wrong time?

Contributions

inspiring meetings involve everyone

Calling a meeting where most people sit entirely silent most of the time makes little sense. Inspiring meetings involve everyone, even if they cannot all speak for long.

Large meetings can be daunting and deter some people from contributing, even if they feel strongly about an issue. Equally, small meetings can inhibit contributions because people feel every word they utter will come under scrutiny. Try breaking participants into smaller groups to discuss an issue for a few minutes, and then invite a response from each person. Alternatively, ask the group to summarise its views, rather than putting the onus on any one person to comment.

If you invite people to arrive with a considered response to an issue, you will also encourage their contribution. You then go round systematically seeking everyone's input. When people contribute, give them your total attention. People soon notice if the manager seems bored or distracted, so stay fully alert.

You can also promote more participation by inviting people to express their objections in a positive, rather than a negative way. Coach everyone to watch out for that destructive phrase: 'Yes but...'.

Handle conflict

It can be scary chairing a meeting – people expect you to handle tension, confrontation and disagreements. Not everyone feels comfortable with this, yet it is all part of becoming a successful manager. How do you tend to react to public conflict? Does it worry you? Is it something you try to avoid or prefer to smooth over? Or do you become forceful, even aggressive. (See also Chapter 3.)

The secret of handling conflict in meetings is straightforward. First of all, allow it to surface. Having spotted a potential conflict, act positively and ask attendees if they want to deal with the issue on the spot. If so, insist on a full airing of the pros and cons.

Handling conflict, though, also means being willing to deal with feelings. Try asking yourself:

◆ What does the speaker mean, not just the spoken words?

◆ What is the speaker feeling?

◆ What are the other people in the meeting feeling?

These questions can help you diagnose what is happening and to decide what to do next.

Inspire

People look to their manager to hold inspiring meetings, not dull gatherings where routine triumphs over involvement.

You may need to develop ways to lift a meeting, energising people and tapping into their natural creativity so they want to take part. Encouraging full participation can be one way to inspire and another is to keep trying new ways to win people's interest and attention.

New ways to try

◆ Rather than sticking to the same format each time, try experimenting with an entirely new one. For example, you could limit the meeting to one item only and ask everyone to prepare in depth.

◆ Try a fast-and-furious agenda one day, with no item allowed more than say five minutes air time, or invite people to raise their issues by drawing a picture of them with coloured pens or even paints.

◆ Consider holding the entire meeting with everyone standing. One likely consequence is that it will prove admirably short!

◆ Convene the meeting entirely off-site or at an usual place such as a park, a customer's office, an art gallery or a room not normally used for meetings?

Quite simply, use your imagination, and invite the attendees to suggest ways to enliven and make their meeting more rewarding.

Ways to run inspiring meetings

☐ *Invest your personal time in good preparation for your meetings*

☐ *For each meeting ensure there is clarity and good practice about:*
  - *purpose*
  - *attendance*
  - *the agenda*
  - *chairing*
  - *note taking and minutes*
  - *time keeping*
  - *late arrivals*
  - *the environment*

☐ *Make sure everyone can become involved, receiving enough airtime*

☐ *Encourage participation by breaking participants into smaller groups*

- [ ] *Stay fully involved, giving people your full attention*
- [ ] *Coach people to avoid the destructive 'Yes but...' syndrome*
- [ ] *Get comfortable dealing with conflict; allow it to surface and, where appropriate, tackle it head on*
- [ ] *Experiment with ways to lift a meeting, energising people and tapping into their natural creativity so they want to participate*
- [ ] *Keep meetings fresh with new formats, new places to meet and other creative ideas*

18

Encourage creativity and innovation

ERIC SCHMIDT DREAMS OF ORGANISING the entire world's information. Google's CEO estimates it will take his company 300 years to achieve it. With that perspective, Google managers can afford to be extraordinarily patient. They know it will involve constant betting on ideas, without worrying much about the likely return on investment.

Managing for creativity and innovation sits right at the top of Google's organisational agenda. Many other companies also realise that in the longer term, this is the best way to ensure success. Short term they can tweak what they have already. 'Innovation is our lifeblood: we expect everyone to do it', says Procter & Gamble, which embeds it in the whole organisation and does not rely solely on traditional research and development.

Even if you do not feel particularly creative and have never innovated anything, it is still a core part of your management role to harvest suggestions, generate ideas and encourage fresh thinking, particularly within your own team.

But why do so many smart, hardworking managers in well-run companies find it impossible to innovate successfully? Researchers have long puzzled over this situation and blame several culprits such as:

◆ excessive attention on the company's most profitable customers

◆ creating new products and services that do little to help customers

◆ financial tools such as discounted cash and net present value, that underestimate the real returns and benefits of proceeding with investments in innovation.

Often, though, it comes down to some simple factors that you can tackle at wherever you are in the organisation. For example, people often expect innovation to mean some sensational breakthrough that will change everything in its wake. In practice most innovation occurs through a steady application of small improvements, one piled on the other until the cumulative effect of this creativity makes its impact.

Hard work, not genius

you may need to abandon some conventional ideas about being a manager

To encourage creativity and innovation you may need to abandon some conventional ideas about being a manager. For example, it could mean rewarding failure, not having strict targets and accepting loss of control over how people spend their time. IBM summed it up years ago: 'If you want to double your successes, double your failures.'

Creative geniuses usually reject the notion that what they do requires an innate talent, or depends on having the right genes. Twyla Tharp, one of the world's great choreographers and author of a book on creativity, for example, talks of it as a pragmatic, almost businesslike endeavour. She argues it relies on systematic hard work, rather than sudden, blinding inspiration.

To encourage creativity amongst your colleagues you will need to:

◆ capture good ideas

◆ keep ideas alive

◆ find new uses for old ideas

◆ put promising ideas to the test

◆ eliminate blocks that may deter breakthroughs.

All seemingly sensible but, in practice, how do you go about doing them? Here are some of the ways you can be proactive.

Hiring

IDEO, the company that helps clients innovate through design, once interviewed someone with lots of great ideas about computers and the arts. No one knew how to use him, but they hired him all the same. Eventually, he generated an unexpected and highly profitable area of development.

In Maynard Leigh Associates, we have often encountered candidates with strange skills and interests outside our own experience or even immediate needs. Who would have thought, for example, that the man who loved skulls and ferrets would become one of our most valued employees, able to solve most practical problems, from faulty air conditioners, to uncovering strange software for our idiosyncratic requirements.

Imaginative hiring decisions can be a way to promote creativity and innovation in your patch and beyond.

Live with failure

'Please fail very quickly – so you can try again,' is how Google's CEO puts it, underpinning this with ensuring a high tolerance of risk.

Instructed to abandon an apparently unsuccessful display monitor he was developing, an engineer in Hewlett-Packard went ahead and showed it to customers, eventually producing a massively successful product line. Some years later, HP publicly and apologetically awarded him a medal for 'extraordinary contempt and defiance beyond the normal call of engineering duty'.

Living with failure seems the exact opposite of what management is about – bringing order out of chaos. Yet companies with an enviable innovation record allow many flowers to bloom and accept failure as the inevitable price of success.

You probably feel comfortable offering praise and rewarding people for success and penalising inaction. Yet you may also need to get used to rewarding people for failing. Failure is how individuals and companies learn.

failure is how individuals and companies learn

The other side of the coin of living with failure is the constant drive to experiment. What sets

Toyota's culture apart is the way it encourages employees to be forthcoming about the mistakes they make. By encouraging open communications as a core value, Toyota has made its culture remarkably tolerant of failure.

Build innovation into job descriptions

In companies like 3M, P&G, Google, and some Japanese companies, everyone's job description contains a requirement to innovate or be creative. However expressed, whether as constantly seeking improvements or always seeking new ideas, the core message is that everyone needs to be inventive at work. Expecting innovation from everyone, though, works best with satisfied, motivated employees who realise their own managers and supervisors will take their suggestions seriously.

Encourage shootouts

In ITV plc, a 14-person internal unit called ITV Imagine has the remit to incubate ideas or concepts from staff and to gather external knowledge and expertise on national and global trends and technology. As its founder Bruce Robertson puts it: 'We needed to find a way to protect ideas and stop them from being killed off or categorised and narrowed.'

One of the most vital ingredients to look for in assessing and pursuing new ideas is who has the energy to pursue them. If you cannot decide which new projects or new ideas to bet on based on objective data, at least select on the basis of ones that have the most committed supporters.

You can promote creativity and innovation by encouraging situations where ideas must fight it out in public. This is not the same as encouraging personality clashes or relationship conflicts. Instead, you make people present their ideas for public scrutiny and get people arguing about them.

Challenge the structure

Toyota's competitors famously excused its success on, first, an undervalued yen, then a docile workforce, followed by Japanese culture, and finally superior automation. Eventually, though, came the realisation that Toyota had learned how to gain more from its front-line workers than other companies. It used a disciplined process for turning them into problem solvers, innovators and change agents.

Gary Hamel, author of a farsighted book on the future of management, takes an informed and highly-critical view of conventional management. He argues that the best managers in the future will be those who know how to innovate, finding entirely new ways to lead, co-ordinate and motivate.

Management innovation allows companies to reach new levels of performance and differs from basic product or service innovation. It challenges convention but requires discipline to succeed. For example, how much freedom do your people actually possess to try new ways of doing things? Are they so constrained by rules and conventions that there is little chance of anything more effective and productive emerging? How could you bend the rules, alter the constraints, release the energy to invent? What might be getting in the way of them becoming innovators? If you do not know, try asking them. Invite them to explore with you what it would take to release their potential to come up with new ways of working, thinking and doing.

Look for the obstacles that your organisation erects to stop or slow fresh thinking, experimentation and the willingness to fail. Having identified them be active in trying to minimise or eliminate their effects. A 2008 global study by the Hays Group found most executives (80 per cent) say innovation is a top three priority but only one in five say they feel able to do it.

You could also face an uphill struggle to encourage creativity and innovation if your organisation unwittingly creates blocks to breakthroughs. In most companies, innovation remains the exclusive job of certain individuals, while only about 6 per cent are innovation democracies in which everyone gets a chance to be creative and make breakthroughs.

Spotting

From penicillin to Post-it Notes so many breakthroughs arise from people seeing possibilities, rather than the actual innovation itself. Spotting new ideas and realising their

hone your spotting skills

potential can be as important as devising the ideas in the first place. Great spotters always outperform actual creators. No matter how creative you can be personally, the world will always produce far more ideas than any single individual will. So hone your spotting skills!

The first step in honing is staying deeply connected with the core purpose. What do you want innovation to achieve? What is the need for it? Why does it matter so much?

Many great innovations die because no one makes a connection between the idea and its eventual outlet. To spot great ideas waiting to explode look for the following.

Unexpected happenings

These can be highly productive sources to prompt new ideas because most people dismiss them as accidental, disregard them or resent them.

> *Use the unexpected as a trigger for creative discussion and ways to relook at 'how we do things round here'.*

Incongruities

Gaps between expectations and results can be a rich source of fresh and innovative thinking. The famous invention of the Post-it Note stemmed from the failure of the original glue to work as expected.

> *Use 'what went wrong?' and 'what can we do about this?' as triggers for new thinking.*

Industry and market changes

Structural changes can offer opportunities for innovation almost overnight. The fortunes of many dotcom companies, for example Amazon and the social website evolution, stemmed from this realisation.

> *Keep reviewing how shifts in the environment offer new ways of behaving and being and have implications for existing products and services.*

Demographic shifts

This can generate innovation opportunities, as these changes, while heavily data driven, still need imaginative interpretation.

Realising an ageing population meant it would become harder to recruit young people, companies like B&Q have innovated by hiring older workers, well beyond normal retirement.

Take known demographic trends and extrapolate them a few years into the future to assess their likely impact on the organisation, and what it does and how it does it.

Changes in perception

Changes in mood, beliefs and attitude can offer enormous opportunities to innovate.

As the mobile phone evolved into an everyday object that everyone should own, it provided a large arena for companies to innovate and use their creativity. A trend against disposable plastic bags offered new opportunities for existing companies to both save on packaging and sell longer-life bags.

Look for current alterations in perceptions as a place to explore the opportunities to innovate and change.

Revealing stories

These can be a great source of creativity and innovation.

When you hear of an inspiring story at work, what does it tell you? What lessons does it suggest for the future? How could you use this to generate some new action or direction?

Managing the creatives

It is far easier to kill creativity than to support it. Not because of a vendetta against it, but because organisations love coordination, productivity and control. These develop their own momentum that can unwittingly crush new ideas or experiments.

Some managers also fear creativity and what it may unleash. To spark innovation you may need to rethink how you and your colleagues respond to it, motivate, reward and assign work to people.

Managing the bright sparks

- Acknowledge their knowledge – make them feel special while making sure they stay connected.

- Win resources and give them space – clever people want and need these to succeed.

- Be an umbrella – help the bright sparks cope with the organisational bureaucracy, shielding them from its worst excesses.

- Congratulate failure – clever people live on the edge of failure, not all innovations work.

- Give direction – make sure your bright sparks do not disappear up their own goals; help them stay related to those of the organisation.

- Listen to the silences – getting the best from them requires you to develop your situation-sensing skills; that is, the ability to assess morale, commitment and individual motivation.

◆ Be accessible – listen hard to the needs of your bright sparks. Your message should be: 'I am available and you are important.'

◆ Encourage outside recognition – they cannot live by internal appreciation alone. They are encouraged by recognition from outside, for example by awards for the best research paper and so on.

◆ Simplify the environment for them – all organisations have rules but bright sparks thrive under an absence of rules and the rules need to be agreed, for example those involving risks.

◆ Don't expect gratitude – clever people often resist leadership, so do not expect thanks for getting it right.

◆ Discover people's inner passion – both to solve problems and do things they believe are new and worthwhile.

Finally, beware of compulsive idea generation. Mobilising huge amounts of innovative thinking and constant creative chatter seldom delivers practical organisational results. For purposeful action, make sure there is a steady focus on implementation. In short, stop people just talking about it and start doing it.

Ways to manage innovation and creativity

☐ *Use imaginative hiring decisions*

☐ *Reward those who insist on doing things their own way and like being different*

☐ *Allow your people space and time to explore ways of being creative and innovative*

☐ *Provide situations where new ideas must fight it out in public*

☐ *In making sense of new ideas examine who has the energy to pursue them*

☐ *Search out and destroy, or try to minimise, the blocks to creativity and new ideas*

☐ *To promote new thinking start with a problem that has large consequences, and one that stirs the soul*

☐ *Search for opportunities that offer potential breakthroughs, such as unexpected happenings, incongruities, industry and market changes, demographic shifts, and changes in perception*

☐ *Review how you motivate, reward and assign work to people – do these encourage or deter fresh thinking?*

☐ *Manage your creative talent to maximise its effectiveness*

☐ *Deter excessive talk about creativity and help people focus on doing it*

19

Select and recruit

'WE LIKE MR FRIENDLY, Mr Ambitious and Mr Faithful, but we don't like Mr Grumpy, Mr Lazy or Mr Dishonest,' explains MD John Timpson at a HRD conference. He was talking about his firm's approach to recruitment (reported in *People Management*, May 2008). The company tells its interviewers to associate a candidate's personality with a character similiar to that from the Mr Men children's series. Timpson's unusual approach probably works a lot better than many of the conventional recruitment techniques companies employ. The company knows who it needs to recruit and wants everyone to be sure about how to do it.

If you happen to be a manager in one of the most successful companies in the world, which of course you may well be, recruitment and selection will almost certainly mean 'getting the right people on the bus'. This is far more proactive than simply filling the occasional vacancy and emerged from a seminal study into how truly outstanding organisations and their managers approach selection and recruitment (see *Good to Great* by Jim Collins). What all these companies had in common was their unwavering commitment to finding and hiring the right people, and *only then* deciding on exactly where they wanted the bus to go: that is, what they most wanted the company to achieve.

Doing it well

To get the right people on the bus though, many organisations often continue an unhappy tradition of poor recruitment practices. As Henry Stewart, founder of Happy, a leading IT training company and winner of several best employer awards complains: 'One of the things that really gets me mad is that most recruiting is absolutely terrible' (*People Management*, 20 March 2008).

What exactly goes wrong? Basic errors include:

- not knowing who you need to recruit
- not knowing why you need to recruit them
- overreliance on interviews for selection
- excessive trust of reference checks, or making none at all
- use of highly dubious personality tests
- poor interviewing skills.

Consequently, many appointments fail to live up to expectations. That is putting it mildly. In fact, an estimated half of all senior-level appointments end in a firing or resignation and at lower levels the record may be even worse. One reason for such bad outcomes is excluding the right talent in the first place.

Wasting half your available talent seems so obviously wrong, yet entire countries, let alone companies, still do it. Unwilling to see half the nation's potential wasted any longer, in early 2006 the Norwegian government made a dramatic decision. To avoid the risk of dissolution, it became mandatory for public companies to change the composition of their boards in favour of more women. The country subsequently set a global record for the highest proportion of female non-executive directors (The *Guardian*, 6 March 2008). Around the developed world managers complain they cannot find the right talent, while ignoring the potential already available to them both within and beyond the organisation.

Outside recruitment agencies now often handle the administrative chore of creating a shortlist. While apparently a cost-effective approach, it may also cut you off from spotting talent that does not fit neatly into the job description to hand. Because of their passion to 'get the right people on the bus' the best managers take a close interest in the recruitment process.

the best managers take a close interest in the recruitment process

The process

Faced with a vacancy in your team you may naturally be anxious to fill it. Yet this may miss the bigger picture, since sensible recruiting starts with the organisation's, or a division's, business plan. From this flows the rest of the process.

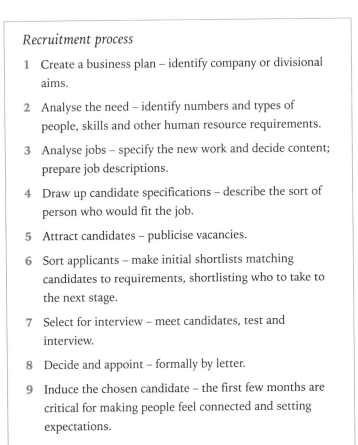

Recruitment process

1   Create a business plan – identify company or divisional aims.

2   Analyse the need – identify numbers and types of people, skills and other human resource requirements.

3   Analyse jobs – specify the new work and decide content; prepare job descriptions.

4   Draw up candidate specifications – describe the sort of person who would fit the job.

5   Attract candidates – publicise vacancies.

6   Sort applicants – make initial shortlists matching candidates to requirements, shortlisting who to take to the next stage.

7   Select for interview – meet candidates, test and interview.

8   Decide and appoint – formally by letter.

9   Induce the chosen candidate – the first few months are critical for making people feel connected and setting expectations.

Why recruit?

By holding the bigger picture, you position yourself as able to think and act beyond your immediate role. It means pursuing answers to questions such as:

◆   What does the organisation want to be?

◆   What are its aspirations?

◆ What is its strategic intent?

◆ What future capabilities will the organisation need?

These help focus on the strategic aspect of recruiting. International research consistently shows a large proportion of people at work feel underused, disengaged or alienated. The figure can be as high as 8 out of 10 employees who feel underused. The results suggest the value of a strategic approach where you first look hard for the resources you need from within, even when it means developing them to the level required.

There is also research evidence that star performers brought in from outside seldom live up to expectations. So, apart from the above strategic questions, your initial recruitment question needs to be: 'Do we have someone internal who can do this work?' While offering fresh energy, expertise and perspective, outsiders take longer to adjust to the prevailing culture than those recruited internally. If you are trying to change culture though, external people may fit in more easily.

Who do we need?

Failure to get the right person on the bus often stems from confusion about the sort of person needed, which is why the slightly bizarre Timpson approach mentioned earlier makes sense. At least the company seems clear about people it does *not* want to employ.

Lengthy job descriptions with their lists of tasks seldom prove decisive during actual recruitment. Instead, aim for a broad, yet accurate, picture of the *intent* behind the job.

What do you want this person to do? What are the essential areas of responsibility? For example:

◆ manage the help desk and ensure it deals promptly and well with all requests

◆ handle all press enquiries and build good relations with the media.

Short, clear work descriptions, rather than pages of tasks, will best support your recruitment process.

Check also whether the prevailing recruitment system treats everyone who applies with equality and respect. For example, does everyone contacting the company in search of a job always receive a friendly reply? Are job adverts worded so they attract all available talent?

even when issuing a general rejection check on its approach

Finally, even when issuing a general rejection check on its approach. Does it show respect and perhaps wish the person good luck in their search for another job, rather than a few clinical lines of dismissal?

The interview trap

Most managers believe they are good at interviewing even though research evidence suggests otherwise. One reason is that unstructured interviews prove to be poor predictors of success when used as the main means of hiring. Rather than relying mainly on interviews, some organisations take prospective employees through a condensed, two-hour training module to see if the candidate can support others and has the potential to learn and train colleagues.

You can increase your chances of selection success by using the following long-standing guidelines.

◆ Structure interviews into a logical sequence covering key areas.

◆ Rather than relying on attitude questions, such as 'How do you feel about... ?', instead ask behaviour and situation questions, such as 'What would you do if...?' and 'How would you deal with...?'

◆ Identify those critical questions that can rapidly exclude or include someone: for example, 'If you were offered the job would you take it?'

◆ Avoid relying solely on the interview as your main means of selection.

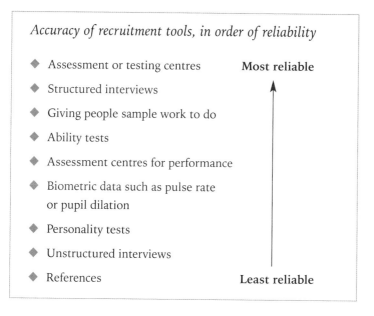

Accuracy of recruitment tools, in order of reliability

◆ Assessment or testing centres   **Most reliable**

◆ Structured interviews

◆ Giving people sample work to do

◆ Ability tests

◆ Assessment centres for performance

◆ Biometric data such as pulse rate or pupil dilation

◆ Personality tests

◆ Unstructured interviews

◆ References   **Least reliable**

Interviewing seems easy because apparently you merely fire questions at your victim. In practice, most people need to develop their interviewing skills to gain confidence, reduce bias and avoid the halo effect (see below).

Spot the liar

The 2008 winner of *The Apprentice* reality show publicly admitted lying in his CV. Unfortunately for the cause of integrity, being untruthful in this case did not prove fatal to his selection.

Imagine you have three fresh CVs in front of you. How many will contain lies and inaccuracies? According to a 2003 study by the Risk Advisory Group, of CVs submitted by job applicants, two out of three cannot be fully trusted. To spot dodgy CVs look for gaps in the person's life story, then dig into the accuracy of claims made about skills, knowledge or qualifications.

Even without the CV, there remains plenty of scope to mislead during an interview. But the body cannot lie, and you will often be able to detect candidate cover-ups. For example, listen for negative statements such as 'I am not an anxious person', rather than 'I am a calm person'. Be alert for missing details, for instance not volunteering names or gaps in their story. Follow up on short answers. For instance, responding 'Quite a lot' to 'What do you know about our company?' may hide ignorance if there is no elaboration.

Watch also for physical clues such as squirming in the seat, a lack of hand gestures, continual touching of the nose, excessive eye contact and a general increase in the number of speech errors and nervous tics.

Verbal clues to help you to root out deception include:

◆ how long the candidate takes to answer questions – liars
  generally go on for longer

◆ slow and very considered speech – the candidate is
  thinking ahead, perhaps to avoid self-revelations (though
  watch out for someone suffering from a speech defect)

◆ fast, high-pitched speech as way of glossing over
  something

◆ anxious to fill in pauses between questions, as if having
  something to hide.

Generally, the less prepared someone is for an interview the
more they will reveal the tell-tale signs.

Generic questions

Anti-discrimination legislation and the
requirement to ensure fairness means you
need to become fully aware of what you can
and cannot reasonably ask in an interview.
As a general guideline, you can ask anything
so long as it is central to the person doing
the job effectively.

*you can ask
anything so long as
it is central*

To develop your structured interview, create a focus on
some, or all of the following issues.

◆ Ability in current or past positions – does the person
  have the technical skills to handle the role?
  'Describe your working day.'

'What are your three most important responsibilities in your present or last position?'
'Tell me about a problem you found difficult to handle and why?'

◆ Ability to adapt – how flexible is this person?
'Can you give examples of where you have changed in response to situations at work?'
'Describe a time when your boss asked you to do something that initially seemed beyond you, and what you did.'

◆ Motivation – what drives the candidate?
'What personal qualities will you need to make a success in the job you are applying for?'
'What have you done in your current job that you are most proud of?'

◆ Communication skills – does the person have the necessary interpersonal skills, especially for roles interacting with customers, whether internal or external?
'Tell me about a time when you went out of your way to satisfy a customer, a client or a colleague at work.'
'What departments do you have day-to-day dealings with?'
'What difficulties have you encountered, and how did you handle them?'

◆ Decision-making skills – does the person show they can make sensible work choices, no matter how limited their role?
'Tell me about an unpopular choice you have made at work.'
'What kinds of decisions are hardest for you?'
'Describe a situation where you needed to think on your feet or adapt quickly.'

◆ Organisational skills – the ability of the candidate to
   organise their workload productively.
   *'Tell me about a goal you set recently, what have you done to
   reach it?'*
   *'Describe a time when you failed to reach a goal; what did you
   learn from that?'*
   'What do you do to relieve stress at work?'
   'How do you go about planning your day?'

◆ Coolness under fire – can this person handle stress and
   show composure when under pressure?
   'What is the most difficult situation you have faced?'
   'How did you react?'
   *'Tell me about a situation where there were objections to
   your ideas.'*
   *'Tell me about an occasion when your performance did not live
   up to your managers' expectations – how did you handle the
   criticism?'*

◆ Manageability – is this person likely to respond well to
   being managed?
   *'When your manager gives you directions what is your general
   reaction?'*
   *'What are some of the things about which you and your
   manager disagree?'*
   *'In what areas could your manager have done a better job in
   managing you?'*

◆ Candidate preferences – what kind of management style
   does this person respond to best?
   'How did your manager get the best from you?'
   'Describe your manager's strengths.'

'Tell me about the best manager you have had; what made this person exceptional?'

◆ Loyalty – does the candidate have a sense of duty to their employer, not just servile loyalty?
'Tell me about a time when you felt it necessary to convince your team to do something, such as change a policy or procedure.'
'How did you go about this?'
'Has there ever been a time when you went along with a policy you did not agree with? Why?'

◆ Self-assessment – what is the candidate's self-perception and how did they arrive at this judgement?
'How would you describe yourself?'
'What motivates you and why?'
'What are your plans for future study?'
'Give me some examples of mistakes you have made in your job; what have you learned from them?'

◆ Interest in the job – how keen is this person to come and work for you?
'What attracts you to this position?'
'What interests you most about us?'
'Why did you apply for this role?'
'What do you know about our company?'

Halo and goodbye

A candidate walks in wearing stylish clothes and talks in an accent suggesting an expensive private education. Depending on your own background, the immediate impression you gain may colour every other conclusion you draw about this person, and perhaps quite wrongly. This is an example of the halo effect at work, in which unconscious errors or bias can influence your entire view of a candidate during selection.

The halo effect shapes perception because we make inferences about purely subjective qualities. We assume a well-dressed person must be competent or that 'nicely spoken' means they are nice to people they deal with. Both these may be entirely untrue. So, to counter the halo effect, concentrate on objective factors that can help screen out subjective influences.

the halo effect shapes perception

Fairness

Even if your organisation has a sophisticated HR support system, take responsibility for ensuring that the recruitment process you become involved with is fair. In particular, be alert to issues of diversity and the need to avoid discrimination of various kinds involving race, sexual orientation, age, gender and disability.

Discrimination and diversity can be tricky and complex areas and there are numerous guides available on these issues. Before attempting to get the right people on the bus, make sure you understand the constraints.

Ways to select and recruit

☐ *Take a close interest in the recruitment process*

☐ *Use strategic questions as part of your recruitment role*

☐ *Review whether and how the business plan relates to the decision to recruit*

☐ *Before recruiting, check whether someone internal could do the work*

☐ *Assess whether you could eliminate, or redistribute the work*

☐ *Develop your interviewing skills in a safe learning environment*

☐ *Avoid relying solely on the interview as your main means of selection*

☐ *Structure interviews into a logical sequence covering key areas*

☐ *In interviews, use behaviour and situation questions, not just attitude questions*

☐ *Identify critical questions that can rapidly exclude or include someone*

☐ *Develop skills to spot clues to root out candidate deception*

☐ *Learn to spot the halo effect, which distorts perceptions of candidates*

☐ *Be aware of discriminatory recruitment practices and how to ensure equal opportunities and encourage diversity*

20

Persuade and influence

THE NEW PHILIPS ELECTRONICS CEO Jan Timmer presented his senior team with a dummy newspaper, post-dated by seven months, headlined: 'Philips declares bankruptcy.' As his stunned managers stared at the figures, their disbelief turned to anger, then realisation that only drastic cost-cutting would avoid bankruptcy. Within three years the company had radically improved its performance.

Effective managerial and leadership performance depends on the ability to persuade and influence. Sometimes, as Jan Timmer showed, it may mean administering a shock to shift people's thinking and attitude.

With declining scope to force people to conform, almost anything you wish to achieve depends on your ability to persuade. Organisations today run largely through cross-functional teams of peers. These do not thrive on unquestioning obedience. People not only ask 'What shall I do?' but also 'Why should I do it?' It seldom works to play the 'Because I'm your boss' card.

Persuasion itself has a mixed reputation. It is often associated with the dark side of communication:

◆ propaganda – telling people what to think

◆ half truths

◆ flattery

◆ reciprocity – doing and obtaining favours

◆ loaded language

◆ repetition

◆ manipulation of feelings

◆ false comparisons

◆ conditioning or indoctrination – making people internalise an ideology

◆ generating fear

◆ group pressure

◆ creating cognitive dissonance – offering conflicting ideas that must be reconciled.

Yet, in some form, these play a part in various ordinary human endeavours. Insurers, for example, create fear of accidents, illness, or death and then offer solutions to reduce anxiety.

See it from their point of view

Persuasion is all about getting people to do something they would not necessarily do. Persuasion means being able to see things from another person's point of view, answering that often unspoken question, 'What's in it for me?' The answer may not necessarily turn out to be entirely self-interested. For example, people may be motivated to do something because they think it is the right thing to do, rather than because of some financial reward.

Surveys of best workplaces show that while tangible benefits, such as discounted bicycles or a subsidised restaurant, can be persuasive, what affects people more are the intangible ones. For instance, the reassurance of knowing what is going on or the pleasure of being part of a team.

So how well do you understand the aims of those you want to persuade? Do they really grasp what you want to do, and is there any conflict between the two?

To persuade your audience make your message as concrete as possible. In bidding for a contract to rebuild station waiting rooms, the winning design company invited its potential clients to hear its proposals. The clients were deliberately kept waiting in a dirty room strewn with empty coffee cups and stale sandwiches. Moments before the clients rose to leave in a fury, the design company team entered to explain this experience was similar to what the rail company's passengers suffered and what their designs would address. By making the message concrete and giving the clients an actual experience the bidders proved highly persuasive.

make your message as concrete as possible

To sharpen up your message in response to 'What's in it for me?' use the three 'whys?' technique. Keep asking 'Why?' in response to the question 'What's in it for me?' After three whys? you will have deepened and further clarified the core message.

Know your audience

When trying to influence bosses and colleagues, many managers typically rely on a one-size-fits-all approach: for example, do the research, make a case and argue strongly to gain acceptance. But treating your target for persuasion as a deep thinker, for instance, makes little sense if they mainly work through scepticism, being suspicious of every piece of information that challenges their world view.

Likewise, when trying to persuade someone who is risk averse, it will be hard to win their agreement if you assume they welcome risk. Or take the person who likes to make decisions based on how other trusted colleagues make decisions. Because they are afraid of making the wrong choices, such a person will probably not warm to arguments relying mainly on pure facts and analysis.

Persuasion, therefore, works best through treating it as a process tailored to each particular situation. Putting it more crudely, you have a much higher chance of gaining agreement by knowing which buttons to press. Discover people's criticisms and try to understand their negative reactions. See this as giving you important information, as a symptom of something you need to understand more fully.

Reframing

When people see what you want to do in a negative light, the challenge becomes how to help them view it differently while retaining the essence of the basic message. This calls for reframing.

Reframing offers new ways to express a situation so it becomes more acceptable to those on the receiving end. It may also challenge negative thoughts based on evidence, offering a more realistic picture of the situation. For

reframing may also challenge negative thoughts

example, 'I think this report is too long and the points are not clear,' can be reframed as, 'It's obvious you have put a lot of effort into this, I'm really impressed. Maybe you could put the main arguments early on and highlight them in some way. Well done.'

Having talked about 'the exciting changes ahead of us' and found that people respond negatively, you might instead reframe by talking about 'the new opportunities for personal growth or advancement'.

Reframing sometimes demands adjusted phrasing so people become more willing to hear your message. Examples include: 'it is a challenge, not a problem', 'it only happens to really special people', 'you will have some great stories to tell about that', 'some people would pay for that kind of experience'.

It is more likely you will need to adjust your message to create common ground between you and those you want to influence. Reframing may also offer a face-saving mechanism.

To reach this common ground means unravelling the nature of people's objections. For instance, in trying to persuade a top team to agree to the company's acquisition, the buyer reframed the original proposal differently, insisting a purchase would only go ahead if there was a true meeting of minds.

Successful reframing relies on achieving an emotional connection, where the other person feels moved in some way to alter their position. This happens, for example, when a leader inspires people to do something they might otherwise be unwilling to do. The process may also break down the whole task of persuasion into smaller, more manageable chunks. Instead of seeking a huge shift in the other person's perception or behaviour, you identify a series of small changes that together add up to what you want to happen. For example, if you encounter resistance to giving approval to your new project, it might be better to reframe it as 'let's do a feasibility study' or 'what I really would like to suggest is a trial period'. (See the persuasion pyramid on page 268.)

Use authority

Conveying authority can be incredibly persuasive. Think about where your authority comes from. Does it stem mainly from your managerial role or perhaps your expertise, your ability to draw on extensive experience or who you know, and so on?

Managers usually overestimate their own authority, believing that their role has built-in authority based on power. Yet this may not be the case at all. Research from Ashridge Business School suggests authority or credibility is more influential than power itself. But what happens if your authority is weak? You could:

◆ hire others to bolster your position, such as bringing in a consultant or recognised expert

◆ use outside sources of information to build your posi-
    tion, such as using respected external reports, provide
    lectures by experts or circulate articles by specialists

◆ launch pilot projects on a small scale to show the value
    of your ideas and demonstrate your expertise.

Extend your influence

Though authority allows you to exercise influence, you can
seek to extend it by analysing the factors affecting it.

First, draw these three circles on a large sheet of paper.

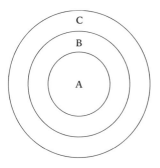

Secondly, in the centre list those issues you believe you can
affect with *no* outside assistance. Thirdly, in circle B add
issues over which you or your team have some, but not complete influence. Fourthly, in outer circle C add issues beyond
your sphere of influence. For example, you may have no
obvious influence over the agenda of the top leadership
team, or what some other division in the organisation
chooses to develop in the way of new products or services.

In the final stage, explore creatively how you might expand circles A and B to increase your influence over the forces affecting a situation.

An influence map, which charts the various stakeholders involved and shows their relationships to each other, can also be a useful way to become clearer as to who you need to influence. A real-life influence map, amended to preserve confidentiality, appears opposite.

Build common ground

This is part of the reframing approach already mentioned. You present your arguments so they appeal strongly to those you are trying to persuade. It's all about identifying shared bene-fits and answering that key question: 'What's in it for me?'

Through good listening, testing your ideas with trusted colleagues and questioning those you want to persuade later you can unravel how best to create the common ground you need. Often, such activities will spark a sudden realisation of what it will take to create a persuasive case and change people's minds.

Use vivid language plus compelling evidence

effective persuaders use language in a particular way

The most effective persuaders use language in a particular way. They bring the facts and numerical data to life with examples, sto-ries, anecdotes, metaphors, analogies and personal experiences. Above all, they make the message concrete in some way.

Influence map

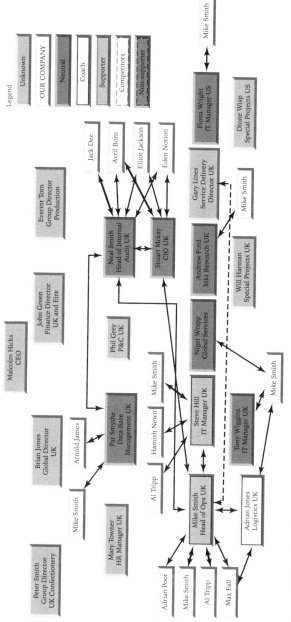

Legend

- Unknown
- OUR COMPANY
- Neutral
- Coach
- Supporter
- Competitors
- Non-supporter

Peter Smith Group Director UK Confectionery

Malcolm Hicks CEO

John Green Finance Director UK and Eire

Everett Torn Group Director Production

Brian Jones Global Director UK

Mary Towner HR Manager UK

Arnold James

Mike Smith

Pat Smythe Data Base Management UK

Phil Grey P&C UK

Neal Smith Head of Internal Audit UK

Stuart Mckay CIO UK

Jack Dee

Avril Born

Elliot Jackson

Eden Notion

Al Tripp

Hamish Newn

Mike Smith

Steve Hill IT Manager UK

Nigel Wrapp Global Services

Andrew Ford Mkt Research UK

Gary Lines Service Delivery Director UK

Mike Smith

Fiona Wright IT Manager US

Mike Smith

Adrian Poor

Mike Smith

Al Tripp

Max Fall

Mike Smith Head of Ops UK

Adrian Jones Logistics UK

Tony Wiggins IT Manager UK

Mike Smith

Will Harman Special Projects UK

Dione Wisp Special Projects US

Notes: 1 Names changed to preserve confidentiality.

2 Colour version distinguishes between a coach, a supporter, a neutral and non supporter.

Stories are particularly powerful when you want to persuade. Through a compelling tale, you make the listener live through an experience and tap into all kinds of responses ranging from sudden understanding or inspiration, through to a new level of empathy, and so on.

The more vivid the story the more people will relate to it and consequently your ability to influence them towards the behaviour you want increases. Effective persuaders unleash the power of language.

Stories let you convey compelling evidence without antagonising the audience or encouraging it to fight back. By only relying on compelling facts you invite people to argue, debate and criticise. This may be fine for an abstract discussion but it may do little to persuade people to take action or buy into what you want them to do.

A good story, using vivid language and incorporating compelling evidence, will engage your audience and therefore become highly persuasive. It is not enough, though, to tell a story. It has to match your agenda and bring to life your core message, not merely be a piece of entertainment.

Connect emotionally

If you come from a technical background or specialist expertise, you may believe that all it takes to persuade people is sharing the facts. Surely, the evidence 'speaks for itself'? Purely factual evidence seldom proves decisive in persuading people. Impressive flow charts, tables and spreadsheets often leave audiences unconvinced. They cannot connect with such impersonal material.

Strong persuaders know that feelings sway people and they become emotional matchmakers by using the following.

◆ **Commitment** – Persuaders show their dedication to what they advocate. If you do not appear to care strongly about what you want to happen, why should other people?

◆ **Insight** – Persuaders develop an accurate picture of their audience's emotional state. Using this they adjust their arguments to meet people's needs. Knowing what moves their audience they make sure they give it to them.

◆ **The unexpected** – Persuaders surprise people with their message, through how they communicate it: for example, with a gripping story, or an unusual way of presenting a vital piece of information.

Use the persuasion pyramid

Aristotle long ago argued that persuasion needed three ingredients: character and reputation; emotional appeal; and logical arguments. These still apply, though we now know a lot more about techniques for getting people to change their minds.

While building your persuasion case, you may find it helpful to use the persuasion pyramid overleaf. It can prompt you to be flexible when creating your persuasion message.

As noted earlier, some people mainly respond to **logic**, relying on facts and arguments. Others, though, respond best to new ideas or a particular angle on an issue (i.e. **creativity**), which you need to discover when building your persuasion argument. Nearly all successful attempts at persuasion also need to reflect people's beliefs and feelings. **Emotion** plays a key role in helping you connect with those you want to persuade.

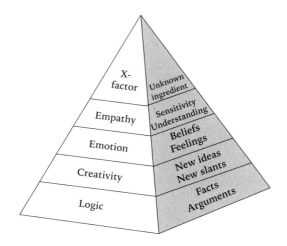

Empathy is the ability to recognise how people feel. You put yourself in their shoes and demonstrate sensitivity and understanding about an issue.

the X-factor can transform your persuasion impact

Finally, the **X-factor** can transform your persuasion impact. By definition, it starts as being unknown and may require some ingenuity to uncover. Once you find it though, it may prove the key to altering people's minds. For example, a top team's reluctance to adopt a new form of technology may dissolve when you reveal that several company competitors have already done so. Or an ambitious colleague who needs to improve their presentation skills may accept help when you offer to watch their next presentation.

Non-persuaders

◆ **The hard sell:** Using persistence, logic and exuberance, managers push their ideas to a close. But this simply gives opponents something to grab onto and fight against.

◆ **Resist compromise:** Too many managers regard compromise as surrender. But it is essential as part of constructive persuasion. People want to see the persuader is flexible enough to respond to their concerns.

◆ **Present great arguments:** Arguments alone are only part of the equation that change minds and persuade (see the persuasion pyramid opposite).

◆ **A one-shot effort:** Persuasion is a process, not an event. Usually it involves listening, testing a position, developing a new position that reflects feedback, more testing, incorporating compromises and then trying again.

◆ **Not hearing:** Listening plays a key role in persuasion since you need to take into account people's reactions to what you want to do.

Finally, you do not have to do it all yourself. If you do not know how to persuade or influence those you want to, look around for someone who can point the way, who has the knack or the right contacts.

The brick walls you hit will not necessarily keep you out or stop you getting what you want: they merely test how badly you want something to happen.

Ways to persuade and influence

- [ ] *See it from other people's point of view*
- [ ] *Know your audience*
- [ ] *Use reframing to present your arguments differently in a new context*
- [ ] *Use authority*
- [ ] *Extend your influence*
- [ ] *Build common ground*
- [ ] *Use vivid language and compelling evidence*
- [ ] *Connect emotionally*
- [ ] *Use the persuasion pyramid to develop a flexible persuasion strategy*
- [ ] *Watch out for non-persuaders, such as the hard sell*

Last word

IF YOU HAVE WORKED YOUR WAY THROUGH the 20 ways to survive and thrive, or at least the ones that seem most useful, you are well set for tackling the management role, at least in terms of information. You will find many further reading suggestions at the web page mentioned at the start of this book: **www.20ways.dpgplpc.co.uk**. However, knowing the most is of course no guarantee of rising the furthest.

The experience of successful managers reflects less the acquisition of knowledge, and more their ability to invest constantly in personal growth and development – of themselves and others for whom they are responsible. Managers start to atrophy once they cease being open to opportunities for personal growth, or no longer take a close interest in the development of those who they manage. Continuously investing in your development is the only sure way to succeed as a manager, which does not necessarily mean forever attending formal learning events, though these too can contribute.

Regularly monitoring your own development and reviewing what needs to happen next can help pace your management career. For example, by staying alert to your development needs you will know when it seems sensible to seek promotion, make a sideways move or perhaps leave for greener pastures. You can undermine an otherwise sound record of achievement by staying too long in one place, after you have exhausted the scope for personal adjustment and improvement.

When you finally quit your current role for new challenges, what you leave behind and the people you have developed will shape people's judgement of your overall success.

Best wishes for your future as a manager and leader.

Sources

BELOW ARE SOURCES for various points made throughout the book. They are not necessarily suggested as further reading although readers may want to use them as such. For a comprehensive list of recommended further reading please visit *The Secrets of Success in Management* website at: **www.20ways.dpgplpc.co.uk**.

Introduction

Collins, Jim (2001) *Good to Great*, Random House

Hamel, Gary (2007) *The Future of Management*, Harvard Business School Press

Leighton, A. (2008) *On Leadership*, Random House

Chapter 1

Goleman, Daniel (1996) *Emotional Intelligence*, Bloomsbury

Takeuchi, H. *et al.* (2008) 'The Contradictions that Drive Toyota's Success', *Harvard Business Review*, June

Chapter 2

Barwise, P. and Meehan, S. (2008) 'So You Think You're A Good Listener?', *Harvard Business Review*, April

DeVito, J. A. (2005) *Messages: Building Interpersonal Communication Skills*, Pearson Education

Chapter 3

Jones, G. (2008) 'How the Best of Best Get Better and Better', *Harvard Business Review*, June

Chapter 5

Ibarra, I. and Hunter, M. (2007) 'How Leaders Create and Use Networks', *Harvard Business Review*, January

Chapter 7

Drucker, P. (2004) 'What makes an effective executive', *Harvard Business Review*, June

Chapter 11

Collins, J. (1994) *Built to Last*, Century
Brad Gilbert's comment is from 'Listening leaders focus on coaching', *The Listening Leader's Newsletter*, 2 November 2005, International Listening Leadership Institute

Chapter 12

Kennedy, G. (2008) *Everything is Negotiable*, Random House
Malhotra, D. and Bazerman, M. (2007) 'Investigative Negotiation', *Harvard Business Review*, September
Sebenius, J. (2001) 'Six Habits of Merely Effective Negotiators', *Harvard Business Review*, April
Sun Tzu on *The Art of War*, translated by Lionel Giles, **www.bnpublishing.net**

Chapter 14

Ghosal, S. and Bruch, H. (2004) 'Reclaim Your Job', *Harvard Business Review*, March

Heath, C. and Heath, D. (2008) *Made to Stick*, Arrow Books

Chapter 15

Sirkin, H. *et al.* (2005) 'The Hard Side of Change Management', *Harvard Business Review*, October

Chapter 16

O'Connell, A. (2007) 'Decision Making, Hotter Heads Prevail', *Harvard Business Review*, December

Chapter 18

Coutu, D. (2008) 'Creativity Step by Step, A Conversation with Choreographer Twyla Tharp', *Harvard Business Review*, April

Hamel, G. (2007) *The Future of Management*, Random House

Hamel, G. (2008) 'The Why, What and How of Management Innovation', *Harvard Business Review*, February

Lyer, B. and Davenport, T. (2008) 'Reverse engineering Goole's Innovation Machine', *Harvard Business Review*, April

Sutton, R. (2001) 'The Weird Rules of Creativity', *Harvard Business Review*, September

Chapter 19

Collins, J. (2001) *Good to Great*, Random House